THE
MATERNAL
EFFECT

THE MATERNAL EFFECT

LESSONS ON THE IMPACT OF A MOTHER'S OLD FASHION AND FUNDAMENTAL VALUES

SYLVESTER CARRINGTON

CITIOFBOOKS, INC.
3736 Eubank NE Suite A1
Albuquerque, NM 87111-3579
www.citiofbooks.com
Hotline: 1 (877) 389-2759
Fax: 1 (505) 930-7244

Ordering Information:
Quantity sales. Special discounts are available on quantity purchases by corporations, associations, and others. For details, contact the publisher at the address above.

Printed in the United States of America.

ISBN-13:   Paperback   979-8-90124-442-5
             eBook   979-8-90124-443-2

Table of Contents

Dedication

This work is dedicated to the memory of my mother, Iola Mayers, and her contemporaries in Roebuck, whose values positively impacted my life as a youngster, and continue to guide my behavior and outlook on life even today.

Acknowledgements

A debt of gratitude is owed to some very influential persons for helping bring this project to a successful conclusion. Kudos to my friend Leila Nicholls-Springer for having the presence of mind to arrange the event back in 2016, when we welcomed the opportunity to congratulate and celebrate, with the distinguished seniors of our neighborhood that sacrificed and paved the way for the success of so many. That event was the inspiration for this work. Thanks again, Leila. A very special word of gratitude is extended to the many seniors who showed up and participated in making that Sunday afternoon event successful.

I also thank my friends, Leila, Randy Phillips, Lionel Lynch, and Drs. Ingrid Jones, Kathy Purnell, and John Mills for taking the time to read the manuscript for the purpose of producing brief blurbs on how it affected them. I thank you very much for your candid remarks and appreciate your willingness to contribute in a meaningful and significant way.

My wife, Hortense, deserves my heartiest thanks for the hours she spent reading and re-reading the manuscript, editing, suggesting, and correcting along the way. Additionally, I am grateful to her for writing the preface to the work, a treatise that is both appropriate and powerful, and sets a welcoming tone for our readers. Your dedication is admirable.

Preface

I am delighted that my husband has finally capitalized on his long-held desire to write a book on the values that his parents, especially his mother, lived out every day for him to observe. What is more delightful is his focus on the importance of modeling values to children when they are young and more receptive to learning.

He, like many others, has been fortunate to be the recipient of first-class modeling by the most important players in the arena of modeling positive and life-changing values, principles, standards, and expectations. Common and well-known cliches like the one that says parents are our first teachers, or another regularly quoted one, "it takes a village…" are more than catchy themes. They are factual.

Research suggests that the ages between two and seven years are the most critical for learning new skills and knowledge. While the learning of values is not specifically mentioned in the research findings and conclusions, it is safe to conclude that children and youth of this age range that are exposed to a daily display and modeling of parental values are equally susceptible.

Without a doubt, parental values transfer easily an naturally. It is not difficult to observe and arrive at a conclusion concerning the values that are important to parents and those in leadership positions, responsibility, and influence where children and youth are concerned. They repeat behaviors they value over and over, a process that influences youngsters, bombarding them with positive modeling, reinforcement, and high expectations; thereby creating a positively charged environment that encourages children and youth to internalize the behaviors they observe before claiming them as their own.

Parents who value good health, exercise often and regularly prepare healthy meals. Those that value home organization and cleanliness, practice them daily and reinforce these behaviors constantly. The teacher who values fairness, makes it a public daily display in the classroom, on the playground, and in her instructional and grading behavior. The police officer that values non-violence and racial equity, works hard to repeat these qualities in his dealings with the public. Likewise, moms and dads that value clean language, model the expected standard every time.

The point is that parents are dispensers of values. The specific values they deem important for transfer to their children are consciously practiced, repeated, modeled, and expected. They understand that regular repetition of desired behaviors eventually becomes habits, and habits turn into values.

You are about to embark on a journey with the author. A journey in which he carefully walks you through his experiences as a youngster, observing the constant modeling of specific values and expectations by his mother and other adults in his small and closely-knit childhood neighborhood in Barbados, his island home; behaviors and values that he has personally adopted, that shaped his character, his development, and his way of life.

The goal for you, the reader, is to compare your own values list that you treasure, and think about what you have done, or are doing, to model, transmit, and dispense them. On the other hand, you may want to list those values that you may have acquired from your parents, church leaders, teachers, or a particular neighborhood resident. I also hope that you take the time to complete the Extended Value-added Thinking and Action exercise at the end of each chapter.

Enjoy!

Hortense E. Carrington, MA, Educator (retired)

Introduction

I was in Barbados in June of 2016 for a television interview on *Mornin Barbados* and a book signing event for my second book, *It's Your Word Against Mine*. A few days later, I, along with several residents from Roebuck, the small village of my birth, and residents from the surrounding neighborhoods of Indian Ground and Rock Hall, attended a program at Indian Ground School, where we received our primary education when we were small children.

The occasion was a celebration and thanksgiving event that was hastily and impulsively planned and organized by my friend, Leila Springer, and I, both residing in North America. She resides in Toronto, and I am in Georgia. It was Leila's brainchild; her thinking and brainstorming concluded that since I was going to be in Barbados to promote my book, and since she was planning a vacation visit to the island that would coincide with mine, that we set aside approximately two hours to celebrate and recognize the academic and professional achievements of our little school, its alumni, and especially the senior citizens of neighborhood that had contributed and sacrificed so much on our behalf.

Surprisingly, the attendance was very encouraging and beyond our wildest expectations, indicating that the senior citizens, the middle-aged, and even the youth, were extremely proud of their scholars and achievers. Secondly, the attendance that Sunday afternoon was a silent confession that a celebration of this nature, and on such a public scale, had never happened before, and that what we were doing was appropriate, and even long overdue.

Obviously, one or more questions may be lurking in the mind of the casual reader, but I'll address the most obvious. Why was there a celebration and thanksgiving event to recognize local scholars, high achievers, professionals, and residents of this particular neighborhood, when brilliance and exceptional academic achievement are commonplace in small villages and obscure districts all over Barbados? The response is not only simple but may be historical and cultural as well.

First, I was surprised and more than a little disappointed and even embarrassed when on the aforementioned television show, I learned that the hosts and nobody else on the set had ever heard of Roebuck. It was a question for which I was totally unprepared, simply because I was sure that they would have done some simple research before the show to at least have a cursory knowledge of the place, especially because a copy of the book was made available in sufficient time before the day the interview was scheduled to air.

But it quickly turned into a lighthearted moment as I relished the opportunity to engage in a brief instructional session on the location of my birthplace. At least, it was a moment of personal vindication and validation. Just before sending the book off to the publishers, I intentionally and purposefully edited the subtitle to read *How Words Express the Cultural Traditions of the US and Roebuck, St. Peter, Barbados.* It was time to put Roebuck on the map, so to speak.

While the above assumption may hold some merit, it can be argued quite successfully that Roebuck, Indian Ground, Four Hill, and the other surrounding and relatively unknown districts held a significant role other than the agricultural ones mentioned previously - a thesis that will be articulated a little later.

When I was growing up in Barbados in the fifties and early sixties, it was common medical practice for physicians to make house calls. I distinctly remember Dr. Gilmore, a short Caucasian man with his small medical bag and rather quick steps, responding to calls from the neighborhood. He was in and out of the patient's house in what seemed at the time too minimal a stay to administer effective medical service. But that is how it appeared to me at the time. Fortunately, Dr. Gilmore's services were not regularly needed because the people of Roebuck were usually in robust health. Needless to say, neither Roebuck nor Indian Ground, or Four Hill, for that matter, had a locally born and bred doctor that we could proudly call our own. Medical services, like many others, were imported.

Truthfully, a similar situation existed in education. Most of us attended The Indian Ground School, where lessons and instruction in reading, writing, and arithmetic were delivered by headmistresses and teachers who resided outside the immediate area. Headmistress Alma Paris drove in from Speighstown, and her replacement, Ms. Maynard, traveled all the way from St. Michael. Ms. Redman was from nearby Benny Hall; Ms. Nicholls came in from The Whim, and Ms. Williams was from Diamond Corner. In short, our early teachers, like physicians, were not home-grown. They were brought in. They performed a valuable service and left for their own neighborhoods at the end of the day. The practice was repeated day after day for years and decades.

But Roebuck, Indian Ground, and the other small villages in the immediate vicinity either appeared pleased with the status quo, or they may have been patiently waiting their turn; waiting for the day to come, when one person would break through the existing dearth — the unbreakable glass ceiling; the day when at least one local student would qualify to work in an office in Bridgetown, or in a bank in Speighstown; or even work as a teacher at Indian Ground School. The strategy appeared to have been centered on the thinking that the breakthrough would eventually and naturally emerge, and that a pattern and a revolution would be set in motion once a starter was found, and that Roebuck, Indian Ground, and Four Hill would begin to consistently produce students and professionals with qualifications and expertise of the caliber mentioned above.

As luck would have it, just as the biblical verse, *"Can any good thing come out of Nazareth?"* lifted from John 1:46 was applicable, that glimmer of hope that Roebuck was looking for showed up on the horizon. Rixford Marshall became a policeman. My sister, Elaine, started teaching briefly at Indian Ground School before transitioning to psychiatric nursing. Similarly, Gweneth Marshall began a career in nursing, and Shirley Ramsay went into teaching at The Indian Ground School, attended Erdiston Teachers College, and later assumed the headmistress position at the local school.

Amazingly, the long-anticipated momentum has not ceased and may even be getting stronger. To date, Roebuck has produced several high-profile professionals: two medical doctors, Ambrose Ramsay and Gabrielle Scantleburry, an attorney in Kim Ramsey, and a deputy postmaster general in my cousin, Dorcas Scantleburry, to mention only a few.

Next door in Indian Ground, Doriel Best worked as a civil servant in the Internal Revenue office, while Leila Springer added an international flavor when she became a published author and the Executive Director of the Olive Branch of Hope, an organization based in Toronto, that is devoted to advocacy, awareness and support for women experiencing breast cancer.

I am taking you back to the celebration event that was mentioned earlier. I was sitting on the stage with the other speakers, anxiously waiting my turn to address the gathering, when a startling revelation suddenly and forcefully hit me. I admired some of the special people sitting appropriately in the front row. Ms. Watson, Ms. Halls (Morris), Brother Nick, his wife, Viterose, Rita Ramsay, and Theophilus Holder were all there. Their ages ranged from the mid-eighties to the mid and late nineties. They sat there with pride and accomplishment, graciously taking in the proceedings.

For me, it was a moment of personal reflection. Noticeably absent were some very important dignitaries that had a positive impact on, not only my young life, but on the youthful experience of many of us that were present that Sunday afternoon: The Sobers family, The Marshalls, The Scantlebury families, The Blackman-Ramsay family, The Strakers, Harold and Doris Worrell (my maternal grandmother), Milton Best, Dorothy Redman, my first teacher, had all passed on a long time ago, but their memories and the impact they had on me as a youth were seriously and emotionally overwhelming.

It was then that my attention shifted from focusing so much on the achievers we were there to recognize, to the dignified seniors, parents, grandparents, and role models sitting up front and center. It was quite coincidental that they sat in such a prominent place, but I couldn't help but think that they were exactly where they belonged: up front and center.

After all, that was the position they steadfastly occupied in our upbringing for many years. This was their moment; their time to shine; their time to be honored. Needless to say, a wave of emotion washed over me as I privately basked in the excitement of the moment, while waiting for my turn to give my address, feeling confident and fortunate that I was a recipient of their support, guidance, and sacrifice.

Something good did come out of Roebuck, I reminded myself only moments before I was introduced by my friend, Leila. And they were sitting there for all to honor and admire, not even thinking of themselves as the 'something good' I referenced earlier. And it was at that late moment that I decided to make significant alterations to my prepared remarks to focus on this special group instead of the gifts, skills, talents, and achievements of many of us for whom the celebration was organized in the first place.

"Your mother would have been proud of you," Leila managed to tack on at the end of her introductory remarks. Suffice it to say, I was already in a fragile emotional state of mind, and had to fight extremely hard to maintain control in the early moments of my speech. Of course, my mother would have been proud of me. More than anyone else, she almost single-handedly provided the motivation, environment, and whatever else it took to land my siblings and me in the academic and professional standing we proudly occupy today. Just like Ms. Morris and Golda did for their children. And how other parents like Theophilus and Joyce Holder, Rita Ramsay, Kareen, The Watsons, The Scantlebury families, The Blackmans, The Marshalls, The Headleys, and The Strakers did for their children.

That Sunday afternoon, I spoke on the theme *Our People, Our Pride, Our Possibilities,* choosing to focus the major portion of my address on the Our People part of the theme. I remember mentioning how our parents and the other senior residents worked in the hot sun in the cane fields and in the potato and yam grounds on Sedgepond Plantation, from early in the morning to late in the afternoon, when they *knocked off* at the sound of the bell; how they made sure that we worked alongside them when we were out of school; and how the young boys had responsibilities for caring for the sheep and the cows, making sure that they were taken out to graze before we went to school in the morning, and going back after school to bring them in for the night.

I intentionally took the time to go into great detail, recalling memories of long ago when we were children, how our never missed work in the fields and on the plantation; how they appeared to take enormous and personal pride in performing such a lowly job to perfection, and with absolute satisfaction; how they did not have the luxury, or the right to put in for a sick day, a personal leave day, a mental health day, or for an annual vacation. And I made sure to articulate it emotionally and thankfully so that those elderly dignitaries understood that those of us with earned doctorates, and those of us that had prestigious law degrees, enviable MD degrees, as well as those among us that had made a name for themselves with accomplishments as teachers, and carpenters, nurses, pastors, priests, construction workers, authors, university professors, postmaster general, civil servants, and even the administrator of a world-renowned Breast Cancer organization, were there to pay tribute to them in an official and public forum.

I concluded by reminding them that even though some of their fellow pioneers had already passed on to their rest, and because they wanted something better for us, that it was because of their relentless and unselfish sacrifice on our behalf that all of us were thankful recipients and beneficiaries of their noble and gracious gift. I reminded them that as a result of their 'something better' mantra, I, and those with me, were now able to enjoy the blessings of sick leave, personal leave, and vacation time - privileges, rights, and freedoms that were not available to them.

The one thing that was most astounding about the entire affair that Sunday afternoon was the apparent level of peace, and the degree of contentment that oozed freely and uninhibitedly from each of them as they sat there basking in the comfortable atmosphere, rich with the praise and adoration that were thrown their way. They appeared to be living vicariously through the accomplishments of their children, grandchildren, and the products of Roebuck and Indian Ground that had made something of themselves. They clearly conveyed the impression that they had done their job on our behalf and were satisfied and pleased with what they had accomplished through us.

As I surveyed their faces, the message I got most convincingly was the one that said, "We have received our reward. We knew all along that you could be anything you wanted to be; that something good could come from Roebuck and Indian Ground; that it did not matter where you came from, who your parents were, or whether they were rich or poor; whether they cut canes or dug yams and potatoes on Sedgepond or Burnt House plantations; or whether they were servants in the plantation house; or whether they drove cane trucks to and from Porters or Hayman's cane factories."

Seriously speaking, as I was enjoying the final moments of my remarks that afternoon, the one word that kept floating in and out of my saturated mind, even though I did not mention it in my discourse, was the word 'values.' Right then and there, as I addressed that captive audience in that most precious and poignant moment, it struck me very forcefully that all along, when we were growing up, there was a set of principles, goals, behaviors, and attitudes that guided their lives and ordered their steps. It was an aha moment for me. I had finally come full circle because, at that moment, it was confirmed in my thinking that some basic and simple standards were important to them for generations. And that we were lucky enough to have witnessed those values played out and prioritized before our very young eyes on a daily basis. And how, with minimal formal and direct instruction, those values have directly influenced our lives, our behavior, and our character, and how we have unconsciously copied these principles, made them ours, and used them as a basis and a foundation on which to build a personal vision for our own lives.

Those character-building values include hard work, church attendance, respect for elders, goal-setting, success, family, unselfishness, service, pride in a job well done, schooling, and education. I consciously and deliberately waited to mention schooling and education last on the list of these remarkable principles because I couldn't resist the urge to detail a certain concept that had pleasantly bewildered me for many years. I briefly mentioned it in my second book, 'It's Your Word against Mine,' but I believe it is worth further attention in this context.

It has continued to amaze me all this time how this group of people - our parents, our grandparents, and senior members of our community, relatives and non-relatives alike, latched on to the concept of education on our behalf. In one accord, they let it be known that our schooling was the most vital of all the values mentioned previously. Hard work was a necessary value, respect for elders was demanded, and church attendance was aggressively enforced, but our schooling and its importance took a back seat to none of these.

In all fairness, the fact that they took our schooling so seriously is as stunning as it is unselfish and absolutely intriguing. Intriguing because none of them had even come close to starting high school, far less finishing. For an entire class of people that spent the most productive and professional portion of their lives working on the plantation, or in the plantation house, or planting and harvesting yams and potatoes to hawk their produce in Speighstown, and still had the presence of mind and the unmitigated audacity to will a higher standard and level of schooling for their children and the children of the neighborhood, is parenting of the highest order.

Clearly, they had no sense of what college or university was. I am sure they had never heard of academic language that included the terms Bachelor of Arts, MA, Ph.D., or MD. But you can be certain that if that level of academic vocabulary and professional accomplishment were commonplace in their time and place, it would have certainly been their goal and aspiration for us.

But despite their lack of familiarity with fancy terms and politically and academically acceptable knowledge, their expectations were not shallow, nor were their standards and expectations unreasonable. They nevertheless knew where they wanted us to be, the standard that they wanted us to attain, and the ladder of education they wanted us to ascend to get there. Their goals were simple, tiered, realistic, and practical: go to primary school; sit and pass the eleven-plus screening test; go on to high school; pass some Ordinary Level Exams that were set by the University of London or by Oxford and Cambridge, and get a job as a teacher, or work in a bank, or land a position in a government office as a civil servant, or learn a trade.

That was their strategy. It was left to us to execute. Without a doubt, their unspoken mission statement had to be voiced by my maternal grandmother, Doris Worrell, the very one thrown so many times in my direction. "Go to school, and learn," she would advise. And she never failed to insert the 'and learn' part every time, as if to remind me that I could go to school and not learn.

While the festivities were winding down that Sunday afternoon, a series of last-minute questions popped into my thinking almost simultaneously. It would have been remiss of me if I did not at least give voice to them, if only in conversation with myself. Who will be the dispenser of values now that the elder statesmen and women are finally retiring? Is the series of values mentioned previously still viable and still important? What responsibilities belong to me and to all of us that have been recipients of those examples of good living and unselfish and sacrificial parenting?

Unfortunately, this work does not directly attempt to answer these questions, although some allusions will be made in the narrative and the stories in the following chapters. In all reality, this compilation of essays takes a closer look at the values to which those of my generation were exposed when we were young children and even in early adulthood; the lessons learned, and how they shaped our behavior, our belief system, and even our character.

Chapter 1
Let's Get to Work

All hard work brings a profit, but mere talk leads only to poverty.

-Proverbs 14:23: NIV

And the Lord God planted a garden eastward in Eden, and there he put the man whom he had formed. This quote is lifted verbatim from Genesis 2, verse 8. My mother believed in her Bible, and she no doubt had several favorite verses from both the old and new testaments. But I can tell you from the outset that my mother, Iola Mayers, took this verse not only seriously but literally as well, as if her salvation depended on it.

I am convinced she loved this special verse simply because it had some practicality. She could overtly plant a garden. A kitchen garden. And she did. How do I know that? I was there. I was appointed against my will to help make the garden. Like the Bible says, my mother planted a small garden to the east of our house in Roebuck. Above the house, we used to say back then; above meaning to the east; below meaning to the west. So, our garden was planted to the east of the house. Even though she had limited or no formal exposure to the study of botany, she was shrewd enough to plant the garden to the east, where the lettuce, beets, cabbage, and carrots got the maximum exposure to the morning sun.

Speaking on the subject of planting the garden in a spot where it was certain to catch the sun's energy, it was only one of a

myriad of topics and situations in which my mother and many of her compatriots held such profound knowledge and expertise. It was beyond amazing how they displayed so much common sense in such a vast variety of areas that made life and living so much easier and uncomplicated. They knew exactly which bush to brew when a cold or the flu was coming on, and what concoction of herbs and vines to boil together to ensure we had a complete 'washout' before returning to school after the long summer vacation. No trips to Doctor Gilmore in Speighstown were necessary.

It was that multifaceted knowledge set that they acquired via a combination of culture, experience, and trial and error, that transformed them into creatures of brilliance, wisdom, and authority before our very young and immature eyes. And best of all, the value they so unconsciously passed on to us was that concepts like guidance, direction, and leadership, can be taught by anyone, especially by aged grandparents, uncles and aunties, experienced and locally grown carpenters, seasoned plantation workers, and expert lorry drivers. And that one did not have to finish high school or graduate from college or university with a degree to qualify as a dispenser of information, knowledge, values, and culture.

So, we grew up valuing our old people for the stories they told, the history they passed on, and their sense of duty to family and the local community. They were institutions in themselves. Living legends. And our parents were diligent in expecting us to demonstrate that value in our village's pillars by using overt behavior and specific value statements. I wish I could be one hundred percent confident that the unshakable value we placed on the older residents of our time was still intact and revered by the current generation of children and young adults. It would be a terrible shame if the vast resources of knowledge, culture, heroism, and examples of hard and diligent work were not tapped into and respected, and valued.

I now invite you to pay close attention to the last half of the verse mentioned above because it is terribly important. At least to my mother. She would find her modus operandi tucked away securely in a half verse: "Aand there he put the man whom he had formed." My mother and several others in Roebuck were diligent as far as these ten little words were concerned. Like all other verses in the Bible, this particular verse and these specific ten words were gospel. They packed a huge punch, and it is quite safe to say that they were solely responsible for the direction my young life was about to take.

My mother did exactly what those ten seemingly insignificant words stated. Those words were just a simple statement to the casual or unsuspecting reader. But to Iola Mayers, they were much more. She was a close reader that reacted to her text in ways that others didn't. She probably underlined it in her Bible. It caught her attention, and she followed suit. She put me, the man-child she had formed and birthed, in the small garden to the east of our house.

Be that as it may, the situation got progressively better for my mother. A little later, in verse 15 of the same chapter, God took the man and put him in the garden to dress it and to keep it. To dress it and to keep it. That's the ammunition she needed, for the man is not only in the garden, but he is also now assigned some specific action - dressing and keeping. And like that man in God's garden, I was also destined to become a dresser and a keeper. I would be in good company, with responsibilities akin to those of the biblical Adam. By now, you may have already read between the lines and have undoubtedly inferred that my mother placed a high value on hard, difficult work, and made a conscious effort to pass that value on to me. Not by mere osmosis, or by the show-and-tell method of teaching, but by engaging me in hands-on dressing and keeping.

In actuality, there was another much bigger garden, located much more easterly than the smaller one mentioned earlier. To get to this one, you had to walk east, down to Sedgepond Plantation, about half a mile away from my house. It was here that work, the real work happened. I dare not refer to this much larger piece of land as a farm. A farm gives the mistaken impression that I had a tractor, or a tiller at my disposal, or any other form of farm equipment that is often associated with farming.

So often, I have read accounts of farm work in which the old tractor was fired up, the corn harvester cranked up, and the seed spreader pulled out of the barn at the appropriate time. Not to mention the farm truck, the backhoe, the front-end loader, and the cultivator. My work had to be accomplished by whatever means, with the aid of the hoe, the fork, the bill, the sickle, and the chopper. All powered by the sheer human potential and kinetic energy that gave perpetual motion to my arms and legs. This is the dressing and keeping that gave meaning to the work my mother valued.

For sure, this was hard work. Forking, weeding, hoeing, digging holes, and planting and reaping was hard work. The kind of work that Ben Sasse in *The Vanishing American Adult* termed real work. It was work that exacted a large amount of pain and discomfort; work that drew sweat and encouraged thirst, and brought on hunger; work that made one long for rest in the shade of a spreading banana tree or under a natural canopy made from the tall and leafy sugar cane. And it was not seasonal work. It was work that was, in many cases, daily, continuous and perpetual.

Still, it was not the type of work and pain that jeopardized my health, stunted my growth, or the kind of pain and discomfort that made me a regular in the doctor's office in Speightstown. On the contrary, the work promoted robust health, ensured physical endurance and stamina, and kept me sleek, skinny, and healthy.

But my mother's insistence on hard and real work had little or nothing to do with my health. It was not a priority in her thinking, even though it was important to her that all of us maintain a perfect physical constitution. My physical well-being was only a byproduct of the entire work equation. She valued work and taught me to value it because she ensured it was purposeful. The work was not an end in itself. It was only a means to an end. She valued work on several levels, all of which I continue to value in my adult life.

It goes without saying that my mother was no economist. But on second thought, she was an economist. And she demonstrated this rudimentary knowledge by the value she placed on real work, purposeful work that supported the economy of our home. Tilling the soil, planting and harvesting potatoes, yams, corn, sugar cane, cassava, eddoes, and bananas was her way of keeping the family food budget out of the red; purposeful action on her part that dictated that we spent as little money as possible on foodstuff, depending as much as we could on that work that produced the vast majority of the food that eventually graced our table.

As luck would have it, the soil in the garden to the east, though chalky in nature and composition, was sufficiently fertile and arable enough to produce a vast variety of foodstuff; the richness of the soil probably helped to a large degree by the annual application of the chemical fertilizers, potash and sulfate of ammonia, as well as regular doses of natural sheep dung that we carried in baskets on our heads from the sheep pen under the pandana tree below the house.

A brief mention was made previously of the concepts of producing and consuming. While the work was an important value in itself, many important lessons and incidental byproducts spun off from the work. It appears that my mother, and the others that valued real work, desperately made an effort to impress on us the volume of pride, joy, and usefulness that could be achieved from engaging in real work of this kind; the kind that one experienced when breakfast, lunch, and dinner menus are pulled, dug, or picked from one's own garden that resulted from one's own work; when one can step outside in the backyard and grab a few cucumbers, a handful of tomatoes, a head of cabbage, and a bunch of lettuce to put together a salad on demand; or the sense of accomplishment that one achieved by stepping outside to the fowl pen and returning with several freshly laid eggs to boil, scramble, or fry for the morning meal.

The concepts of consuming and producing are directly connected to the practice and value that are inherent in real work. And the tragedy is that so many do not even understand the relationship between them, far less considering, practicing, and respecting the considerable benefit that can be achieved by marrying them. As I write, I can't help but take a look back at my young life and conclude how fortunate I had been to have experienced broad and constant exposure to the kind of work that afforded me first-hand experience in the practice of producing and consuming; thanks to my mother and her insistence on valuing work.

At the same time, I pity the level of ignorance that is so rampant among so many children, teens, and even some adults, who have had little or no experience with hard and valuable work, and whose education and practice is so limited that they are convinced that the produce, eggs, flour, and chicken, automatically appear daily on the shelves and in the cold storage section of our food stores, and that the only interest they acknowledge is the consumer part they play. They have no idea of how goods are produced and certainly no experience in the work that produces the goods they consume.

It should be no surprise then, that I would be in strong support of any movement or program that has as its goal the creation of opportunities to engage young people in real work ventures that, in turn, help them understand the fundamentals of consuming and producing, and where goods and services are created. Please don't misunderstand me or my premise. I am not advocating that all young people grab a fork, a hoe, and a shovel, head to the backyard to turn over the soil, and eventually plant a garden of okra, beets, and onions. I understand that in many cases, this is not even practical or even possible, and for several reasons, particularly in those cases where land space is unavailable.

On the other hand, I have witnessed creative approaches to gardening on a small scale that have produced the same lessons in the concepts of producing and consuming that I have been talking about. Individuals serious about engaging in real work and in demonstrating how they can be small producers and consumers have constructed wooden boxes, filled them with purchased bags of topsoil, and planted gardens that were the envy of many. Some have even turned a windowsill or two into a miniature garden.

I think this is the appropriate place to introduce a statement as to how the real work I did in my youth followed me after it was no longer compulsory after I came of age and was no longer under my mother's direct supervision; how it subconsciously remained with me when I did not have the time, or the land space to engage in it on a serious scale. After leaving Roebuck for college in Jamaica, I did not have the time to engage in this kind of real work. Honestly speaking, it did not even cross my mind. Sadly, I settled for the position of consumer in chief in the Jamaica years and the years that followed in St. Croix.

In the meantime, I married Hortense, a Jamaican who had also experienced real work in her past. When we moved to Andrews University in Berrien Springs, Michigan, for graduate school, both the resources of time and garden space, which the University freed up, became available. And we (Hortense especially) immediately made use of the opportunity. The soil was terribly fertile, and everything we planted flourished, so much so that we had more than enough for our own consumption, with an abundance left to share with friends and fellow students. The value that was placed on purposeful and real work when we were younger was active again.

We had the time, and the pleasure to observe seeds germinate and seedlings grow to full maturity as the real work in which we invested paid off in a huge way, and the value we had learned to place in this aspect of real work took center stage. Ironically, Hortense almost put our son in the garden as my mother had done for me. One Sunday afternoon, just after we had attended my graduation earlier in the day, we were in the garden getting some beans when my friend, Garford, remarked in Hortense's hearing, "...you are going to have that baby in this garden this very day." Not long after, the first labor pains arrived… an indication that she had her personal work to do. Our second son was born later that evening.

Admittedly, I am not limiting real work to the kind of work I have been talking about so far. Obviously, I referenced this specific work because it is the work that was handed to me and the young men that grew up with me in Roebuck. It is also a fact that I harbor a strong bias in favor of this kind of work because of the myriad of benefits -

economic and otherwise, that it produces. Do I believe it is the best and most effective kind of work for young people? Of course, I do. It goes without saying.

But on the other hand, opportunities to engage the youth in hard and difficult work can be found in factories, some in government and private offices, and others on assembly lines and trash pickup detail. The argument from my perspective is not the nature of the available work, but that all healthy young people should be strongly encouraged to engage in some kind of 'real' work, if only for the personal and other related benefits mentioned above.

Certainly, there are a host of other benefits that can be achieved when young people engage regularly and consistently in real work. Apart from learning and perfecting new and complex skills, there is the social component in which friendships are formed, and the art of verbal communication is fostered and improved. Real work done in association with peers creates an environment that encourages political, religious, and educational conversations. Young people learn to take positions on a variety of social and political policies and current societal issues, and grow stronger and increasingly comfortable at arguing and defending their positions, while simultaneously learning to listen and respect a point of view that is different from theirs.

Similarly, regular participation in the kind of 'real' work that I experienced as a teen is responsible for instilling additional traits and learnings. From personal experience, the work that I did, taught me to endure to the end and to complete a task when quitting was easy. Since then, it has been like transfer of training or transfer of learning that I have recalled and continue to call into service when faced with demanding situations that call for stamina and determination; demanding work, like writing a dissertation, or similar academic and professional demands, even in a situation such as writing this book. Work of this nature helps to build a steely character of endurance, backbone, and independence. "I don't stop when I am tired. I stop when I am done" is attributed to Marilyn Monroe, but the work that I have experienced, and the lessons I have learned from the work, have influenced me to adopt her statement as my personal mantra.

It goes without saying that there is a direct connection between boredom and the absence of real work. "I am bored." I am certain that, if not all of you, most of you have heard this youthful pronouncement time and time again from today's generation of young people. My reaction has always been that I can't recall being bored when I was their age. There was too much to do, even if everything I did was not always productive or purposeful. In retrospect, it seems now that there was always work to do. The saying that the devil finds work for idle hands has certainly been true too many times in my youth.

But boredom for extended periods of time was not the case in my experience, nor was it the experience of my peers in Roebuck. And we did not have the luxury of television, cell phones, and video games. There were too many invitations all around that invited mischief and many more that aroused our curiosity: spending hours catching crayfish with our bare hands in the river, stealing coconuts from the plantation by aiming at them with a stone and watching them fall to the ground as a result of the accuracy of our aim; playing cricket in the street with a makeshift bat made from the coconut branch, and a ball that used to be a milk can, or even a lime, shattering people's glass windows in the process. Girls created dolls out of grass and remnants of cloth, while boys made trucks and scooters out of pieces of wood and leather and empty corned beef cans. Both sexes came together in the dark of the evening for a game of hide and seek before washing up for bed.

Those activities and games were self-directed, and even though they were not considered work, they took care of our boredom, and served as a reprieve from the real work our parents demanded. Their real work assignments charged us with taking out the sheep; bringing in the sheep; gathering wood to use for cooking our food; and carrying buckets of water on our heads from the main standpipe under The Marshall's breadfruit tree, back to our house to be used for cooking, washing dishes, and bathing.

The point I am trying to make here is that even though the real work that was enforced by parental demands was less desirable from our point of view, it was purposeful and contributed to the household economy. In addition, it accomplished what real work was meant to achieve – to provide work for idle hands and to erase feelings of boredom. Ben Sasse asserts that the cure for boredom is curiosity. I agree, but I also believe that real work is just as potent. I have never heard a person engaged in real work complain about being bored.

If by chance, you were doing some close reading of the above paragraph, you would have concluded that my mother believed in scheduling a variety of real work assignments. She believed in variety, ensuring I mastered many skills and gained expertise in others. You already know how she felt about the Bible, how she believed every word and every prophecy, and every story and every parable. She made sure I was in some ways like the biblical Abel in caring for the sheep, the lambs, the hens, and the ducks. And that I had some Cain in me as well, doing real work in the garden, growing peas, ginger, cabbage, and carrots. And if that was not enough, I prepared the pigs' food, served it to them, and cleaned their pens regularly. I retrieved eggs from the bush, left there by wayward hens, and picked pond grass for the sheep to munch on while they relaxed in their pen; and even loaded baskets of their smelly dung on my head, transporting the contents to the garden to the east as fertilizer to nourish our maturing crops.

In addition, my real workload required me to assist in the manufacture of our beds from khus khus grass that grew nearby. In case you are wondering, I was domesticated as well. My mother took care of that, requiring me to do my part inside the house as well as outside. My sisters may disagree, but I did my very tiny share of cooking and cleaning, but took a leading role in painting, scrubbing, and varnishing the floors and furniture.

Consciously or not, my mother appeared to believe that there was a social component to engaging in real work, and appeared to posit covertly that real and painful work, including examples mentioned above, were more beneficial when not performed in isolation. Based on this theory, she always encouraged me to take my sheep out to graze, or *pick* pond grass for them to munch on, or help a neighbor reap and harvest his sugarcane crop, with my neighborhood peers, as if to instruct me concerning the benefits of social interaction and teamwork.

As mentioned before, engaging in real work is never the final or only goal. A wide variety of real work experience is the basis for teaching independence, learning personal responsibility, and creating an awareness of one's strengths, and how acquired skills can be used in the service of one's neighborhood and community. Of equal importance is the realization that Ben Sasse asserts so eloquently. "There is not dignified versus undignified work, nor important versus unimportant," he writes. "There is only useful versus useless work."

I have often wondered if my mother's thinking mirrored Ben Sasse's. She made it known time after time that the real work she had my sisters and I do was not the kind of professional employment she had in mind for us, even though she insisted on the type of work that I had been discussing from the beginning. But at the same time, she knew in her heart that there was nothing wrong with this kind of work. She and her friends valued this kind of work, but when it came to choosing a profession, she wanted something better. If they knew this all along, why did they insist on painful and uncomfortable work? The answer is clear. To teach independence, to learn how to be producers and not only consumers; to acquire the basics of how to take care of ourselves; and how to value and appreciate honest and purposeful work.

Once painful, hard, and real work gets into your system, it becomes almost impossible to dislodge. It becomes an integral part of your makeup or your genetic code. And If you are like me, you must have seen men and women that are continuously busying themselves with real work over and over again. And if you are like me, you would also come to the conclusion that these people have been doing this kind of work since childhood. This is exactly how I felt about my mother and her cohorts in Roebuck. They seemed to know that whatever a person values, he or she does it over and over again. And that's exactly what they did day after day, week after week, for months and years, starting out early in the morning when the smell of bakes frying in many kitchens saturated the early air, when the sun was barely beginning to announce the start of another workday, those brave souls marched to the beat of their own drums without complaint or embarrassment.

Work was their value statement. And it became ours as well, as soon as we, too, learned to value work. My peers, Livvey (Robinhood), Andrew (Foot Pad), Henson (Ice Pick), Sherrod (Dolly), and Carson (Tuckie) were a sturdy bunch. Our health was vibrant, our bodies lean and hard, flexible and supple. In other words, young boys in my day in Roebuck were not feeble, overweight, or sickly, or soft. Or girly. That's what the work did to us and for us. I am not being braggadocious or arrogant. I am simply being truthful and honest. Today, in my late seventies, I am still youthful, strong, and full of energy, and can outwork many that are half my age. Like Kevin Hart wrote in *I Can't Make This Up,* "If you don't believe in your own greatness, no one else will."

I have to indulge in a brief moment of candor that has its origin in my visit back to Roebuck the last time I was there. I came away very disappointed because I did not notice any reminders of the value that was once placed on real work when I was a boy. Most of the gardens were gone, and sheep and goats no longer filled the street in the early morning, on their way to the grazing pastures on Sedgepond plantation, shepherded by young lads.

I didn't see youth that could corral a renegade sow or boar, or that could chase down a runaway sheep like we did when we were called into action. The childhood shrieks of children playing in the street were no longer music to my ears. And the perennial patches of green and lush khus khus grass that were once the raw material we used in the manufacture of our beds were gone forever. Even the simple joy of observing a chick emerging from an egg or the fascination of witnessing an adult cow or sheep give birth to its young appeared to be educational opportunities of the past. In short, it was not difficult to discover that the value placed on hard work was replaced with the passing of time and with the passing of those who valued it.

I spoke earlier of the value of work as it relates to dignified work versus undignified work. Without a doubt, this view of work was the real focus of our parents' value and appreciation of work. It didn't matter the nature of the work to be done. It could have been painting work or cleaning a pig pen work; garden work or housework; taking out the sheep work, or kitchen work. To them, it was dignified work as long as it was not-breaking-the- law kind of work. As long as it was work with a healthy purpose, and as long as it was the kind of work that supplanted the economy of the home, it was the kind of work we needed to do, whether we were teachers, nurses, bankers, or civil servants in the making.

Personally, I took the principle of dignified work very seriously, taking it with me directly into the halls of academia. The story is detailed in my second book, *It's Your Word Against Mine,* but it is worth repeating here. While working on my doctorate at Loma Linda University, I worked at collecting eggs in the chicken house a couple of times a week. It was nasty hard work. It was hot and uncomfortable work. It smelled. I smelled as well as I maneuvered the old, ragged egg carts through the narrow passages, getting stuck in the slush every now and then. It was dirty work, no matter how you looked at it. There was not one clean thing about it except that it met the requirements of the real work that I was used to doing back in Roebuck when I was a young man many years ago. It was dirty work, but it was not embarrassing to work. The work was dignified, just like the work I d I cleaned pig pens at home in Roebuck. I was dignified, even though I did not smell like it at the end of my shift. But I was not ashamed of the work or of myself, a doctoral student. I had done it before. It was purposeful work that supported the economy of my home, my wife, and three rambunctious boys.

After the experience of wrestling with hogs and chasing down wayward sheep when I was a boy in Roebuck, any work beyond that was an upgrade, and I was prepared to do it, no matter what it was, as long as it was honest. It was the brand of work my mother valued as long as it was work that was a means to an end. The nature of the work paled in value and importance to the purpose and usefulness of the task at hand. I had to learn that truth. And I am glad and fortunate that I did.

It was mentioned earlier that the work we did was only a means to an end. It was not an end in itself. And even though we had to do it consistently, regularly, and efficiently, it was not the profession our parents had in mind for us, but the lessons in character building, discipline, and endurance were nevertheless important lifelong attributes that we could take with us into adulthood. And now that I am a parent, I have come to discover that my engagement in real work and the value that I place on work have not gone unnoticed and that, hopefully, I have passed on that value to others, especially to my children.

In addition to the egg-collecting story I told before, I did some other work in graduate school that caught the attention of my children, especially my oldest, Sheldon. In several conversations over time, he has consistently mentioned his witness and his appreciation of how hard I have worked on the chicken farm, cleaning the physics building on campus with him accompanying me some evenings; and working as a security guard at night at Riverside General Hospital. And those who may be familiar with my story might have queried my motivation for engaging in this kind of work, or any kind of work for that matter, especially since I had a full tuition scholarship award due to my position as a graduate assistant. It was the value that I placed on work. That's all it was. A value that was passed on by my mother. It was purposeful work; income that helped to balance the family budget and provide for the basic needs family; the exact lessons on the value of work my mother taught so long ago.

There is one more thing about how our parents and the other adults who had a supervisory position over me and the other young ones in Roebuck looked at work and its role in our upbringing. As mentioned before, our work detail was purposeful, uncomfortable, and at times painful. But there was one thing that the work imposed on us was not. It was never used as a method of punishment or discipline. In one sense, the work was meant to discipline but not in the sense of punishing us for some infringement on house rules. I never heard my mother resort to using work to punish me because I failed an exam. When I failed the very important eleven plus exam, the results of which were to determine which of the best government schools I would attend, my mother did not assign more planting of yams and potatoes in the garden. Nor did she demand that I take extra loads of dung on my head from the sheep pen to the garden to the east. She did not insist that I grab a bill and cut a whole row of sugar cane as punishment when I had a fight with my sister, Elaine.

She was astute enough and sufficiently sophisticated to refrain from associating work with punishment. She seemed to know that had she used work as punishment, that it would have been counterproductive, producing results she never wanted to realize. Hence, her primary goal was for us to learn to value work and not hate it. Imposing hard labor on us would have defeated her purpose in ways that would have been detrimental, even though we were not always in favor of doing the assigned work, or of the time it was to be done.

My parents did not classify their insistence on work as punishment. To them, work was to be viewed as educational and not punitive. Educational, in the sense that the work they assigned was meant to build character, create producers, produce disciplined individuals, and support the economy of the home. As far as punishment is concerned, a good tongue-lashing was always put to use, not to mention the always tried and true belt.

We were not punished by work. Neither were we paid for the work we did. Money did not change hands, either because there were never large amounts of disposable cash available to satisfy a payroll that included my four sisters and me; or because the work was not viewed by my parents as a cash for service contract. To be honest, cash payments were never considered when work responsibilities were distributed. As mentioned before, cash availability was one factor, but the most important side of the equation were the lessons learned in responsibility, preparation for adulthood, doing our part in contributing to the running of the family business, and the joy and exhilaration we so often experienced by successfully completing a project to specifications.

It is not difficult to retrieve that feeling of usefulness and accomplishment that washed over me when I polished the front house floor, varnished the furniture, painted the walls, and cleaned the windows at Christmastime. The house was a festive spectacle. A job well done was enough reward. The thought that the work I was doing should have been performed in return for cash never crossed my mind.

I am sure my sisters had a similar experience. It was not that my mother didn't dole out a dollar here and two dollars there every now and then, but it was never a payment for work done inside the house or even outside. They, especially my mother, also worked as a team at beautifying the outside of our home by using their bare hands, a hoe, or a bill, to dislodge the grass from between the rocks before going to the marl (limestone) hole to dig buckets full of the white stuff, carrying it home on their heads to deposit it in the rocky yard so we could have a 'white Christmas.'

And there was other seasonal work as well. They also had a role in planting gardens; they cooked on an outside fireplace; carried water from the public pipe back home for cooking, washing, and bathing; looked after the chickens and ducks; carried dung from the sheep pen down to the garden to the east, and helped at making our beds out of khus khus grass and flour bags. And in many cases, my mother worked along with us, creating the unspoken mantra that very loudly proclaimed, "We are in this together." Money as a reward was never a part of the discussion.

It was the purposeful and productive work that supported the economy of our home that was preeminent.

So far in this narrative, you may have recognized that I had not used the word chores in the current discussion of the work we were assigned by our parents when we were growing up in Roebuck. There are two main reasons for this very purposeful decision, the first of which is the fact that my parents never used it. It probably was not a word to which they were accustomed, and it was not a word that was stored in their vocabulary. They probably didn't use the word work either. As a matter of fact, they never did use the word work when they gave us our marching orders. The fact is that whether or not they invoked chore or work, we understood what they meant, what was required, and the standard by which the directive would be judged. They spoke in specifics and with simplicity. "Go and bring in the sheep. Go and pick some ripe breadfruit to make breadfruit cou cou. Bring home a bundle of wood when you are bringing in the sheep."

Secondly, the word chores would have tended to conjure up ideas of specificity as far as the work to be done was concerned. One would have probably heard one of us say, "washing dishes is my chore." And another, "sweeping the floor is my chore." And a third would have been heard to declare, "getting water from the pipe is my chore." The truth is that there was some degree of specialization as far as the work was concerned. I was the only one charged with taking out and bringing in the sheep; and with picking up milk each evening from my grandmother's, but for the most part, there were no specific work assignments doled out by gender, age, importance, or interest.

I have mentioned several times that the work my mother assigned us was, at times, uncomfortable and sometimes painful, but always educational and purposeful. I probably should have mentioned this next valued aspect of work before now, but I figure its lessons would be just as valuable and timely here. My mother and others like her, effectively used work as a tool and an object lesson to teach and demonstrate another character-building and valuable component of our upbringing: delayed gratification.

Many times, a work assignment took precedence over a fun or play activity, especially on a bank holiday And I severely hated it at the time. My mother, without fail, would always schedule a work assignment prior to us enjoying a Saturday or day off from school. She often stipulated that some form of work be accomplished prior to leisure time, party time, or merely hanging out with friends. "Work first, play later," she used to dictate in fewer words. That was her encapsulation of the proverb, "All work and no play makes Jack a dull boy."

So, more than a few loads of dung from the sheep pen under the pandana tree below the house to Sedgepond Hill to the garden to the east were in order. Or multiple trips back and forth, carrying buckets of water on my head from the standpipe under The Marshall's breadfruit tree would satisfy the work requirement for the day. To be fair to her, she was thoughtful and caring, stipulating that the work be done early in the morning hours, so that we could have the remainder of the holiday to ourselves

The lessons taught and learned had nothing to do with work or play, although work and play were the raw materials used to get the message out. Delayed gratification is exactly what it was, only that my mother used simpler terms in her explanation. Without a doubt, she believed that play, fun, and entertainment were important themes in our upbringing, but she was quick and decisive in putting them in their proper perspective. She was making sure that the work that contributed to the economy of the home was prioritized.

To her, it didn't make sense for me to be playing street cricket all day, while the garden on which we depended for our food was dying from the lack of fertilizer, weeding, and pruning. Or if there was little or no water in the barrel at home to use for cooking, washing dishes, or general household use, while I spent the day with the guys catching crayfish in the river down the hill in Sedgepond. Her insistence on the delayed gratification technique was responsible for the work getting done quickly and efficiently, thereby preserving the value of work.

Personally, delayed gratification has been a constant modus operandi I have been putting to good use in my own life as a young man, an adult, a student, and a parent, ever since my mother instituted it as an organizational management strategy in our home. As a college student and throughout graduate school, I have consciously used it to prioritize the most important tasks that I had to accomplish. And I still apply the same strategy today: mowing my lawn before settling down to watch television; washing the dishes before relaxing for the evening; and getting some writing done prior to working out in the gym. It is, therefore, not difficult to understand my advocacy in favor of involving young people in work that promotes and encourages delayed gratification. It is one of the tools that prioritizes the work experience for young people, and is directly responsible for helping them develop into organized and successful adults.

There is one last dimension relative to the value that my parents and the other adults in Roebuck placed on the work they did, and the work they expected us to do. They always maintained that the work we did had to be purposeful and that one of its primary purposes was to support the economy of the home, and was purposely designed to turn us into producers and not mere consumers. But beyond that was the work that was done for others. Obviously, they did not refer to this volunteer work in modern terminologies such as service work or service projects, but in retrospect, it is now very clear that to them, service to others was an aspect of work that was valued.

Whether helping a neighbor move a house or pitching in to do their part in helping another resident harvest their crop of sugarcane, they certainly put their muscles, their skills, and their willingness to work on behalf of others, taking me along on many occasions to join in the work that provided an opportunity to be helpful and unselfish. I, along with other youngsters in Roebuck, worked on Saturdays making bundles of sugarcane and carrying them on our heads to a waiting lorry, or to a central location where they were stacked in a heap until they were subsequently picked up and carted off to Haymans or Porters sugar factory.

It goes without saying that this early work-service combination is responsible for awakening in me the attitude toward service outside of my regular profession as an educator. But to be fair and honest, I have not been very active in this area of service as much as I would like to be. However, I remain convinced that young people should be strongly encouraged to engage often in service projects while in school, in college, and beyond. I get excited when I see young people picking up trash, cleaning the homes of the elderly, tutoring students in crisis, going on mission trips, and engaging in work service projects sponsored by their school, community, or church.

I purposefully made the decision to delay a detailed discussion on the character-building value of work until now, choosing to compare my personal beliefs with what the related literature has to say on the topic. I previously mentioned the work of Senator Ben Sasse, and further reading and research very strongly support his theory concerning hard work. Surprisingly, my own beliefs have also been substantially supported by the literature.

The Watchtower Online Library (2005) provides a volume of credible findings on the value of work, and is very specific in its position that work is training for life, as is summarized in the following excerpt. "Extending yourself in physical work, whether swinging a hammer or mowing a lawn, can promote good health. The benefits can go beyond keeping fit and trim: fixing a flat tire, changing oil, repairing a broken window, repairing a clogged drain, and making a bathroom spotlessly clean and sanitary. These are skills that both young men and women do well to know; skills that can help you live successfully on your own one day."

Somewhere in the narrative above, I alluded to the notion that young people and youth can build character by engaging in manual work. I am delighted to discover that The Watchtower Online Library espouses similar thinking. "Hard work can also affect how you feel about yourself." Writing for the US National Mental Health and Education Center, Dr. Fred Provenzano asserts that learning physical tasks can add to your sense of self-reliance and general confidence, and can also foster self-discipline and order, which are foundations to successful employment.

Young people also weighed in on the benefits they experienced as a result of participating in physical work. One young female, Sarah, echoes the following, "Manual labor taught me to be hardworking and industrious. I learned how to be disciplined mentally and physically." Nathan declares, "I learned to enjoy working with my hands. I improved my skills. I saw the quality of my work improve. This built self-esteem."

Another author, Ellen G. White, puts the value of manual labor in a more comprehensive perspective in her writing on the subject. In her book, *Messages to Young People,* she pens the following, "... Each should acquire a knowledge of some branch of manual labor by which, if need be, to obtain a livelihood. This is essential, not only as a safeguard against the vicissitudes of life but from its bearing upon physical, mental, and moral development. Even if it were certain that one would never need to resort to manual labor for support, still they should be taught to work. Without physical exercise, no one can have a sound constitution and vigorous health."

What is truly amazing is the regularity with which the literature mentions numerous character-building terms that are associated with work. The terminology and jargon include confidence, skills, self-reliance, order, self-discipline, hard work, industriousness, self-esteem, discipline, and successful living. It is therefore not difficult to conclude that hard, manual, physical work done by young people is definitely not useless activity. On the contrary, the accepted conclusion is that engaging in purposeful work is a noble endeavor that can be advantageous to young people on so many fronts.

It is obvious that my experience with physical work and manual labor involves taking care of pigs, sheep, chickens, and ducks, as well as tilling the soil, planting food, and harvesting produce. This work was introduced to me by my parents, particularly my mother, before I was a teenager, and a little resentful as I looked at it as mere work, completely oblivious to the hidden attributes that lie in waiting, to turn me into an individual that is molded by the many and sundry character-building virtues listed above.

I am revealing a secret that I have been carrying for many years. I still get fully excited when I see cattle grazing in open fields as I travel to and from Huntsville, Alabama, and to and from Murfreesboro, Tennessee, when I take a trip to visit my son and his family. In fact, close to my house, there is a wide expanse of farmland that is very often the playground for countless heads of cattle. The scene captures my attention every time, and takes me back to those days when I worked with cattle. And the simple occurrence of soil being dug up and turned over by earth-moving vehicles still takes me back to those good old days.

I have always achieved a degree of comfort and pleasure from digging in the soil. Not only has the variety of life forms that make their habitat there amazed and amused me, but the realization that the lab-like depths of the soil are mostly inexhaustible, providing an unmistakable, reliable, and natural source of learning and enjoyment. Who is not fascinated by a wiggling earthworm dancing to freedom as its peaceful place of abode is disturbed? Or by observing the variety of inhabitants scurrying to safety at the jab of a hoe or a fork in their territory?

Be that as it may, I have, over the years, accumulated several object lessons from my vast work experience in soil management and planting. I can't help but compare the deepness of the soil to the layers of complications, impediments, and barriers that are at work to obstruct and impede the plans of so many young people in our day and time, causing so many to lose hope and surrender in frustration and failure, when they have only scratched the surface.

The lesson from this simple analogy is fitting and appropriate. Just as digging in the soil to find that perfect depth and level that is right for planting seeds and saplings, so too is the process and practice of wading through besetments, adversities, and misfortunes on the way to a desired goal or outcome.

Digging has its rewards. The encouragement to the youth and whomever, is to continue digging and tunneling through the deep and dark soils of discouragement, or insufficient role models and mentors, or wading through periods of frustration, and the experience of poverty, failure, letdown, and parental guidance, with the assurance that you will one day arrive at the desired depth and foundation on which to build your future, your profession, or your ambitions. I have been digging in the natural soil for years to plant seeds for food. And with a lot of success. So too, I have dug relentlessly in the academic soil, and in the professional dirt, with similar achievements. The lessons and similarities are striking.

And so, it was with the sowing of seeds: corn, beans, tomatoes, or what have you. It took a while to master the steps in the scientific phenomenon of germination, but with constant practice made possible by my regular work of digging and planting, combined with the hands-on science experimentation of observing the process unfold before my very eyes in a glass jar in elementary school, and later from the expertise of my high school Botany teacher, Mr. Holder, I was fortunate to discover the power that is housed in every seed and kernel.

Without delving into the intricacies surrounding the contents and structure of a seed, as was discussed in Mr. Holder's class, it was rather exciting to discover that the *radicle* always turned down through the dark soil to function as the new plant's primary root system, while the *plumule* always turned upward through the soil towards the light as a shoot, bearing the plant's first leaves.

But as fascinating as the above abbreviated lesson on germination with its fancy and elaborate scientific verbiage might have been, the most captivating occurrence in the process of germination is the fact that no matter the position of the seed in the soil; upside down, downside up, vertical, or horizontal, the radicle always turns downward and the plumule always turns upward. If you have any doubts concerning this botanical truth, try your hand at the tried-and-true experiment of observing the process of germination in a glass jar by placing bean seeds in different positions. It was fascinating to observe the scientific marvel in real time, simply by engaging in hard work. If my mother only knew that her value and insistence on hard work would turn out to be a classroom, with nature as my instructor and teacher.

Is it any wonder that my favorite subject in high school was science, especially those branches that deal with Biology and Botany? And my desire to take and pass my school leaving exams in Biology and Botany is much more than a mere coincidence. Hence, it was an easy decision to make concerning a major to pursue in college, with Biology being my number one, number two, and number three choices. And of all the Biology classes I took in college, my hands down favorite was Plant Physiology. Go figure. And after all that, I ended up teaching high school Biology, which to this day is the highlight of my instructional experience. My mother introduced me to engage in and value hard work at an early age, and her insistence reaped multiple dividends in several aspects of my personal development.

There is so much to learn and several object lessons to glean from the behavior of the radicle and the plumule. As the radicle responds to the pull of gravity and turns downward into the soil; and as the plumule responds to the influence of light and grows upward towards the sun; no matter the position of the seed or the conditions in the soil, each one teaches that no matter our situation in life, and no matter the position in which we find ourselves, young people and others alike, can also make that turn in response to the forces, influences, and persons present in our environment. History is replete with stories of individuals who did just that – made that positive turn, out of less than conducive and advantageous conditions.

It was not the original intention to drag readers through the rigmarole of botanical study. All I wanted to achieve was to disclose some of the lasting and life-changing lessons I garnered from my work experience, and the value I have placed on it. Still, that value did not originate with me. It is a value that I caught; one that was taught by my mother and her contemporaries in Roebuck as they insisted on engaging us in hard, painful, and purposeful work in the fields and gardens.

<u>Extended Value-added Thinking and Actions:</u>

1. Do you agree that work, especially for the youth, is an important activity? Make a list of four or five other values, and life lessons you think are derived from work.

2. Observe young people and even some adults that have engaged in work while growing up. In what ways are they different from those who have never worked?

3. Pull a small group of young people together. List their views for and against work.

4. The author's work experience was the work he did in the gardens and fields. Look around your community and list work and volunteer opportunities and projects that could be done by young people to make it a better place.

5. You are probably a retiree, a professional, a college student, etc. What kind of work did you do as a young person

Chapter 2
Praise and Worship

Church attendance is as vital to a disciple as a transfusion of rich, healthy blood to a sick man.

-D.L. Moody

I am not sure why I mentioned hard work as the first of the significant values that guided our young lives when we were growing up. The fact is that church attendance was just as pervasive and just as seriously valued as was work. As children in our home, church-going was not questioned. To be more exact, it was not even taught. It was caught; practiced and exemplified every Sunday by our parents. Questions of this nature were never asked on Sunday mornings: "Are we going to Sunday school today?" We didn't have to ask. We knew what the answer would be. Always the same. Or, "Can we leave after Sunday school and stay at home for the remainder of the day?" "No, you have to stay for church. And you have to go to the Sunday night meeting. And Monday night service. And to Tuesday night's Young People Endeavor (YPE). And Wednesday night prayer meeting. And Friday night as well."

Sunday was our Sabbath, so the entire day was reserved for church, worship, and praise with a Pentecostal flair: spirited singing that was accompanied by the beat of rhythmic foot stomping and the percussive pulsating harmony of tambourines; and vigorous hand-clapping and swaying and dancing in the aisle. And speaking in tongues. And preaching the Word. The whole works.

Sunday was so sacred that even work of the type mentioned in the previous chapter, except for taking care of the animals, was put on hold in order for us to observe the sacredness of the day. The laundry was not done on Sunday. Men did not go out to fork the soil or cut canes in the fields if it was Sunday. And the women and children purposefully refrained from weeding, planting, and reaping in their gardens. The village shop was closed for the day because Brother and Sister Scantlebury, the initial shopkeepers, and later Ms. Watson, made their way down to church every Lord's Day.

But prior to the worship service, Sunday School was in session. And school it was, in every sense of the word. The curriculum was varied but always relevant and child-centered. There were lectures on how to be good children, bible stories about Noah, David, Moses, Paul, and other biblical stalwarts. And there was direct instruction for sure, in the parables of the sower, the good Samaritan, and the miracles of Jesus on how He turned water into wine, how He fed five thousand people with only five loaves and two pieces of fish, and how He healed a man that was born blind. And if that wasn't enough, memorization of Bible verses and entire chapters was a must. That is why to this day. I can still repeat The Lord's Prayer, Psalm 23, Psalm 34, Psalm 91, and several others verbatim.

The value my parents placed on church attendance went far beyond going to church on Sunday mornings. The value was all-inclusive and reached into other areas and compulsory behaviors that had to be observed, even before we stepped foot in the church.

First and foremost, the body temple had to be cleansed thoroughly before we approached the temple that was made with hands, brick, and wood. Putting it in milder terms, we had to have a full bath before thinking of going to Sunday school and to church. We dared not approach the threshold of the Roebuck New Testament Church of God without taking a full bath, which did not usually happen on the other days of the week, when a half bath was the accepted practice.

Our parents placed too much value on church attendance and what it meant, to allow us to commit that one aspect of the 'unpardonable' sin. They valued church attendance so much that they believed that in order for us to capture the ultimate spiritual value and blessing of church attendance, our natural and defiled bodies had to be physically washed prior to stepping foot into that holy space. They were of the mind that the spiritual cleansing would happen in church, but the prerequisite physical washing had to be accomplished before the service. They appeared to believe that God would have held them in contempt of church and worship if they were derelict in their duty as far as our preparation for church was concerned.

The depth of the value that my parents placed on church attendance and its relation to our cleanliness before going to church on Sunday morning can only be fully understood when one takes into consideration the living conditions at our home. Our house was void of luxuries such as running water and indoor plumbing, conditions that did not always make it possible for us to have a daily full bath during the week. A quick 'wash up' before school and another one before bed was sufficient.

But Sunday morning was vastly different from the other days of the week. Because of the value and the significance my parents placed on Sunday observance, a full bath on Sunday was had by all, in spite of the availability of water. The lesson I gleaned from this is one that has stayed with me until now; that those things one values and esteems are worth fighting for whenever they are not easily or readily achievable.

My parents' value on church attendance was also manifested in a myriad of other ways. Some were minor and unnoticed; others were glaring, planned, and publicly executed with flair and a touch of elegance and class. For example, our dress for church. Sunday was special and valued. Church attendance was equally esteemed, and our appearance had to match in a particular fashion.

Granted, we did not have a lavish wardrobe, but what was special and unique about Sunday church-going clothes was that they were restricted wear that was specifically reserved for the Lord's house. Our Sunday go-to-meeting clothes, usually of finer fabric, were carefully shopped, cut, and tailored to specificity. My parents didn't wear their church clothes to town or around the house, or on casual occasions. Neither could I. Likewise, my sisters. Church shoes, dresses, shirts and pants were not even worn to the annual church-sponsored outings and excursions, or even to church meetings during the week.

At one time, I had only one pair of shoes and a couple of really good shirts and pants. They were my church attire. And for church only. So much so that going barefoot all week was the norm until Sunday rolled around again. Church readiness meant that from head to foot and in between, every article of clothing that covered our bodies was strictly set aside for Sunday and for holy use. Even my hair was cut and combed and styled by my father with a 'part' on the left side of my head, all in preparation for the sacredness of Sunday school and church.

So fixed in my psyche was this parental value that, to this day, several decades later, I still practice the tradition of reserving special clothing for church. And even though my day of church attendance is now Saturday, I continue to hold on to the practice of reserving special attire for church only. I do not dress in my church-designated shirts, neckties, pants, shoes, and suits when I go to work or attend other non-church and socially related activities during the week. And vice versa. I have never worn my home clothes or school clothes to church. Personally, that would have been nothing short of sacrilegious behavior. The biblical recommendation offered by Jesus in Matthew 22:21, *Render unto Caesar the things that are Caesar's; and to God the things that are God's* come to mind.

As referenced earlier, so significant was the value my parents placed on church attendance that it encompassed much more than the actual attendance itself. Like the clothing we wore on Sundays, the parental value of church attendance made its way into another peripheral: the very food we ate. Just as important as church attendance had been, my parents were insistent on how we worshiped. It filtered down to how we ate and what we ate on Sundays. Regulars like salt fish, corned beef, red herring, and even flying fish, staples that graced our table during the week, were taken off the menu for the day and substituted with the more upscale offerings like chicken, beef, mutton, or pork.

It certainly goes without saying that the primary purpose of my parents' relentless value on church attendance was that it would be the catalyst responsible for turning us into God-fearing Christians. Our maturing souls were at stake, and they wanted to be sure that by attending church regularly, the inner transformation they were hoping for would happen to us over time, due to the constant and incessant exposure to the Church's teaching of The Lord's Prayer, and stories like The Good Samaritan, The Crossing of The Red Sea, and David and Goliath, that served as perquisites for the more advanced themes of salvation, baptism, righteousness, forgiveness, hell, and heaven, and of course, the second coming.

But beyond that, the thing that my parents, along with the others in Roebuck wanted the most was that, over time, their children would grow up and mature to value church attendance just as seriously as they did; that church attendance for us would be our own value to treasure and to pass on; not one that was forced and unnatural, but one that was voluntary and genuine. And so it is. My siblings and I still attend church on a weekly basis.

Clearly, the valuing of church attendance has led to other sub-values or secondary values - those that function as appendages to a major value. In this case, our parents' valuing of church attendance has spawned additional values that were not intentional at the outset, but have nevertheless manifested themselves as outgrowths of the parent value. Getting ready for church services on Sunday mornings probably birthed the value of cleanliness, not only for worship but for other occasions as well. To this day, the saying that cleanliness is next to godliness is the mantra that apparently decides our appearance when we leave the house on either a casual or professional mission.

So too is our love for music and singing, another value that grew out of church attendance. We sang loudly and lustily at church, singing one song after another in a rousing song service prior to the sermon. We joined the church choir and performed at the annual Christmas program. When we left church, the singing and the music went home with us and lived with us. And we valued it so much that we would regularly break out in song.

Ironically, my mother, who helped to engineer the church attendance value, could not carry a tune to save her life, but that inability never got in the way of her doing what she could. My father, however, was the master when it came to singing. This was his department, and he relished taking the lead with his strong bass voice and all that went with it. There was no doubt at all that he valued singing and that he wanted to pass it on to us. And we got it. I got it. To this day I still appreciate energetic and zestful congregational singing, simultaneously accompanied by the organ and piano, vigorously joining with my soft tenor voice as I am able.

Much later, my personal value for singing and music was affirmed by one of the most influential individuals in my professional life, Charles Vaughn, headmaster at All Saints Boys School, where I began my teaching career back in 1968. It was evident that he placed a tremendous value on music, and he grasped every opportunity to engage the boys in singing lustily and harmoniously at morning prayers. As I write, I vividly recall this statement he made a long time ago: "If you don't enjoy music, something is wrong with you." I got it then, and I still value it now. It is gratifying to know that nothing is wrong with me. My value remains grounded.

But having said that, I have to admit that the initial unshakable value I originally placed on music has undergone something of a seismic shift over the years, especially since I shifted my day of worship from Sunday to Saturday. The value is still intact, but the genre I embraced much earlier has been eroded and replaced by one with which I am more comfortable. Had I replaced the value in and of itself, there may be cause for alarm, but nothing that dramatic has happened.

Consequently, there is nothing improper about altering or modifying the premise or foundation on which a value is built. I now fully embrace singing the old and time-tested hymns such as *How Great Thou Art, Never Part Again, Tis so Sweet to Trust in Jesus, And Can it Be,* and a number of others that include my favorite, *All the Way my Savior Leads Me,* penned by Fanny Crosby, simply because its lyrics and message accurately match my personal testimony. I hope you won't mind me sharing the first verse with you:

All the way my Savior leads me

What have I to ask beside?

Can I doubt His tender mercies?

Who through life has been my guide

Heavenly peace, divinest comfort

Here by faith in Him to dwell

For I know whate'er befall me

Jesus doeth all things well.

It is obvious that I gravitate to hymns as opposed to the repetitive lyrics that in many cases lack references to God or Jesus and sound more like a secular or romantic ballad than anything else.

At the same time, I wonder how much thought, if any, my parents invested in the possibility of some other intellectual spin-off values, or byproducts that would eventually come to fruition from their insistence on church attendance; those unintended consequences that would eventually break away from the mother value to have a life of their own.

I can say without the slightest fear of contradiction that they did not have the presence of mind to even think of the possibilities that merely attending church on a regular basis could spawn serious intellectual values apart from the ones cited previously. For sure, their only goal, as far as this religious value was concerned, was the development of our moral selves, to save our souls, and to keep us, especially me, out of the street.

One particular spin-off value that emerged from the main value of church attendance, and one that I cherish to this day, is the association with like-minded people, individuals, and groups that share my moral and religious beliefs, as well as a myriad of positions and thoughts on policies, doctrines, church leadership, church politics, as well as politics on the national and local landscape. Like-minded individuals, such as those that are congregants, create an environment that allows for free expression, divergent thoughts and positions, and the kind of support that only a church family can render in times of discouragement, loss, and utter despondency. This is one sub value that I cherish; one that my parents never thought would emerge from theirmajor value of attending church.

Having said that, it should not be interpreted in such a way as to conclude that like-mindedness in a church setting is always a meek and mild state of affairs. Far from it. Discussions and disagreements can be, and have been, downright contentious and disagreeable on a number of topics. In my local and corporate church, there are noticeable differences of opinion among like-minded members, but their opinions are respected. Today, you will find that there are members sitting on opposite sides of many heated and recurring issues that include women's ordination, women preaching, music, the church budget, the wearing of jewelry, the treatment of homosexuals, and even the color of the carpet and floor tiles. I have learned to value the interaction and the uninhibited exchange of ideas in a church setting, a personal development and process that I am sure has its beginnings with the value that my parents placed on church attendance.

Two factors are at work that make a difference; elements that are responsible for maintaining the stability, respect, and tolerance that continue to exist among like-minded people in a church setting. The first is the purposeful and intentional forums and platforms like the weekly Sabbath School sessions, regularly scheduled business meetings, youth meetings, and the like, that provide ample opportunities for like-minded members to agree, disagree, and even argue in rightwing and leftwing discourse while maintaining a level of civility and decorum.

But beyond that is the second and most endearing factor that keeps me and like-minded individuals regularly attending church from week to week. Without a doubt, it is the value that is placed on church attendance. I value attending church, even if it is only out of a sense of habit or obligation, so much so that the happenings mentioned above are not sufficiently potent to dislodge the value that I have built as far as church attendance is concerned. And without a doubt, this was the same depth of value my parents placed on church attendance so long ago, and one that I continue to value to this day.

Nonetheless, I do not want to mislead my readers into believing that I have been the poster boy for church attendance all these years. Far from it. Putting it mildly and truthfully, I am a church dropout. A dropout survivor, but a dropout, nonetheless. And for the life of me, I can't find one specific reason for abandoning church attendance after so many years, especially after respecting it as a personal value, as well as a major value of my parents.

Among the few half-hearted reasons I can come up with include the following: my father migrated to England when I was twelve, and I felt that his influence went with him; I started high school around the same time, and probably felt that it was not cool to go to church any longer; probably my peers also stopped going to church around that time. Whatever the reason, my personal church attendance record took a big hit that lasted for several years.

But my dropout experience does not always run parallel to research findings. The data offers a glimmer of personal comfort in that the numbers say that some seventy percent of young people between eighteen and twenty-two stopped attending church regularly for at least a year, but two-thirds returned to committed attendance. That's according to LifeWay Research (2007). My dropout experience, however, began much earlier, around age twelve, but my return to membership, albeit to a Seventh-day Adventist Church, began around age nineteen when, according to Lifeway, the majority of nineteen-year-olds are heading for the exit.

"Something happens between the ages of 17-19 that accounts for those who leave. Between 17-19 is when the drop takes place," asserts LifeWay. The reasons LifeWay suggests as to why this age group abandons church attendance are striking, not because of a disagreement with the church's theology or out of rebellion. "They simply lose track of the church and stop seeing it as important." As mentioned earlier, this latter finding very closely approximates my experience and behavior as a church dropout.

Similarly, a ten-year study, *Why Our Teenagers Leave the Church* (Dudley, 2000), concluded that between forty and fifty percent of Adventist youth leave the church in their twenties. Interestingly enough, this is just about the exact age when I found myself coming back to church in 1968 when I was nineteen years old. Listed among the reasons young people mentioned as grounds for dropping out are the following: (1) church is irrelevant. They feel unaccepted because their needs are neglected, (2) they feel unaccepted because of the lack of relevant and targeted programs, and (3) the church is oblivious to the reality of their lives.

Honestly, I have no dissension with the findings of either of the two studies mentioned above. On the surface, they appear credible and plausible. However, it has to be said that I did not blame the church as being solely responsible for my dropping out. It was my decision. It was not even a decision. I simply dropped out. At the time, I was probably too young to understand or realize that I had needs of that nature, and that it was the church's obligation to satisfy them. I did not see myself as a needy kid by church standards. On the contrary. I was happy, content, well groomed, and felt quite at home, clapping my hands to the beat of the music and adding my share of participation in the singing. Probably, the only need I might have had was the need to eat, if the service went too long.

Granted, the two projects at the center of the discussion were conducted many years ago; and they were carried out in this country (USA) and may, or may not, have any bearing on the dropout behavior of young people in Barbados. But then again, they may have. It is possible that young people in my native country dropped out of church or are still dropping out of church because their needs are not being met by their individual congregations. What is noteworthy, however, is the reality that I did return to the church to worship with another congregation in 1968 after a six-year leave of absence. What is more significant is the fact that I can count on one hand, with several fingers uncounted, the number of times I have been absent from church on a Saturday since then.

By then, I was certainly more mature to acknowledge that retention relied to a large extent on the attention and interest paid to the youth and the degree of involvement and leadership roles that were entrusted to them. Not that I was actively and intentionally looking for such, or that I intentionally craved it, but it was delivered in large and generous amounts by the leadership, as well as by the senior and well-established members of my new congregation.

Based on the findings of the research projects mentioned, there is reason to believe that there may be one or more reasons why I stayed and decided to realign myself with my new church, especially at a time and age when, according to research, many young people drop out.

I am one hundred percent positive that when my parents insisted on the value of church attendance, they did not think that it would lead to one additional unintended consequence - cultivating life-long friendships. Not necessarily friendships that culminate in dating and marriage, but friendships in general. By the way, if you are like me to think that the majority of married couples meet at church, you may be surprised to learn that this assumption is baseless. According to Wikibooks, the number one place where couples meet is "Other." The assertion is that one-third of couples meet in places where no other couples meet. Additionally, Wikibooks maintains that fifteen to twenty percent of couples meet at school and work, but only eleven percent meet at church.

I have been very lucky to meet and maintain several life-long friendships that had their origin at church or at a church-related establishment. I mentioned earlier that I dropped out of church around the age of twelve and was churchless until I was nineteen years old. It may appear quite strange to say that I still valued church attendance even though I was not attending. The fact that I didn't smoke, drink, break into the neighbors' houses, or drop out of high school to run the streets should be solid validation to support the premise that I had not completely abandoned my religious heritage and the values that I once embraced.

Enter Floyd Marshall, who, along with his mom and sister, Jenny, had the same unwavering value in church attendance that my parents had. The only difference was that Floyd and his family attended church on Saturdays. Their unshakable value in church attendance was demonstrated for all to see. They walked about two miles to church every Saturday morning and repeated the journey, rain or shine, on Sunday nights and Wednesday nights, as well as early in the morning during the week of prayer. Like my parents, Floyd did not keep his value of church attendance to himself, but shared it with me on a regular basis by inviting me to attend his church. Our friendship blossomed on the school bus as we engaged in youthful mischief, but his invitation to attend his church went unheeded for a while.

I was used to passing by Floyd's church as I walked by to visit my grandmother on Saturday mornings. And it appeared that each time I went by, I became more hardened in a promise I had made to myself from way back; that I would never go to a Seventh-day Adventist Church, even though the singing and the music emanating from the small church was so lustily, divine and heavenly.

After all, Saturday was a day I had set aside to revel in my own fun and merriment. I was in high school by this time, and Saturday was strictly reserved for meeting school friends in the city, running cross country, and watching cricket in the park. I graduated high school in 1968, and all of a sudden, Floyd's invitation did not seem so onerous this time around. He invited me to attend a series of meetings, and this time I accepted. To make a long story short, I ended up joining his church and have been a member in weekly attendance ever since.

All of a sudden, the value of church attendance, which my parents highly prized, came roaring back in my personal life. But that value manifested itself in other ways and in other values as well. Our relationship continued to grow as we combined the values of friendship and church attendance, which have been powerful influences in my life, as well as Floyd's, for years. I will address the value of friendship in general in more detail in a future chapter, but it is sufficient to add here that it is a very impressive and selfless quality when an individual not only seeks to befriend you, but also seeks to strengthen that friendship with a desire to see you grow personally, morally, and spiritually as well.

By this time, you may be already aware that in my early years, church attendance for my parents, my sisters, and me, as well as for all the churchgoers in Roebuck, was at a Sunday church, The Roebuck New Testament Church. To this day, I still owe so much to that Church, simply because it provided my first lessons in right living and the very basics in biblical teachings, parables, and stories. Just as important, my attendance and that of my siblings exposed us to human models of morality, uprightness, and integrity, who, by their example, showed us how to order our steps in the community where we lived. In a few words, that was what the value of church attendance was all about.

Likewise, I have also explained my dropout experience from church, only to return to church attendance after many years, albeit to a Saturday-keeping church - The Indian Ground Seventh-day Adventist Church, a congregation with opposing beliefs and conflicting religious practices in a variety of ways. Even so, my parents, siblings, and many more were disappointed in my decision, preferring that my return to church attendance should have been to my former allegiance. But for me, the most significant factor in the whole thing was that I was back, respecting the value of church attendance that my parents had established a long time before. To me, that was the most remarkable occurrence.

The most unfortunate thing that can happen to anyone is to lose sight of a value or a set of beliefs that have been a positive force in one's life for a long time. Most distressing however, can be the complete loss of those value systems and beliefs that were owned by one's family, and you are the one responsible for breaking the traditions and patterns of behavior and beliefs that have been in existence for years.

That was the exact burden I shouldered for so many years. Being away from church not only reflected on my individual behavior, but it was a reflection on my parents and the work they did to show me the value of church attendance. Renewing my commitment to that value was the best thing I could have done, as will be discussed a little later.

For me, church attendance has had its privileges and its rewards. And that value has certainly worked in my favor since returning to Church. I feel bold enough to assert that many of you reading this can testify to, and affirm, the positivity that church attendance has brought to your life, outside of the obvious spiritual blessings. Frankly, both churches have had a significant impact on me in their own unique way, and I have been fortunate to be the recipient of the teachings, the exposure, and the life lessons that bear fruit to this day.

However, what follows next is in no way meant to compare or rate one church as superior and the other as subordinate, but I know I am walking a very fine line when I make this next statement. If I had not aligned myself with the Indian Ground Seventh-day Adventist Church, I doubt that I would have accomplished as much as I have as far as my educational and professional standings are concerned.

I have always sought to keep company with individuals who have built a sterling and reputable record of moral, educational, and professional behavior, taking very seriously the proverb that says, "You are the company you keep." Just as true is the maxim that teaches this next truth, *Chances are that if you keep the right company, you will likely end up in the right place.* I am again convinced that many of you have experienced this concept time and time again. And I certainly have, in and out of the church setting. But since our immediate focus happens to be on the latter, it is appropriate to maintain that focus for the present to elaborate fully on the matter of being in church at the right time, with the right person, and how the events that transpired on one particular Saturday were responsible for initiating a life-changing chapter in my experience that continues to unfold to this day.

Here is the story. It was 1971, and by this time, I was in my second and final year at Erdiston Teachers' College. I lived on campus during the week and commuted home on the weekends, attending Church on Saturdays. This was my weekly habit. On this particular Sabbath, with the pre-sermon preliminaries out of the way, I was more than anxious to give my full attention to the visiting preacher for the day, Pastor Everett Howell, the youth director from the Church's headquarters in the city.

I should add here that at that point in my life, I had already decided that I would be through with formal education when I graduate from Teachers' College a year or so later. As far as I was concerned, I had achieved above and beyond the level I had set and way beyond the achievements my parents had for me. I had made them proud. I had made myself proud. I was done with school. Period.

But I was soon to discover the nature of this line of thinking is dangerous as well as counterproductive, because it stifles opportunity-seeking and self-advancement, when one concludes that he or she has arrived at the limits of their intelligence, creativity, and ability. More than that, I see it as an insult to our Creator, who has blessed us with an extensive endowment of mental and creative genius; a gift to invest in a myriad of challenges and opportunities.

That wasn't my thought process at the time. Even though, at times, I was impressed with the degrees my tutors and professors had, and even admired them and the skills they possessed, I was still determined that I had come to the end of my journey of formal education. I distinctly remember one of my tutors writing the different kinds of doctoral degrees (Ph.D., Ed.D., etc.) on the board in one of my classes, and my personal and silent reaction went something like this, "I want one of those." Still, my determination not to further my education persisted.

That was until Pastor Howell announced his sermon title for the day, "Christian Education." My ears perked up, and my attention was one hundred percent acute and intense as the Pastor went into full exhortation mode on the benefits of education; how the Seventh-day Adventist Church had colleges and universities all over the world; and how the Church's educational system of private education was large, second only to the Catholic system; and that the system delivers education from kindergarten to doctoral programs.

This was news to me. The information he imparted made a deep and personal impression while providing its share of utter discomfort and unease, as it appeared as if he was speaking specifically to me, gazing directly in my direction, and telling me that he was aware of the decision I had made about aborting my educational opportunities, and that he had come to invite me to rethink my decision.

Wrapped in attention, my mind still found time to wander, but not too far off. I told myself that I had been attending Church for years and that this was the first time I had ever heard a sermon preached on the value of education. It goes without saying that I had sat through sermons on sin and salvation, hell and heaven, the first and second resurrections, and the first and second coming. But never a sermon on education. It was as new as it was fascinating. My decision was up for review.

It was the next thing the preacher said that put the decision to review my intentions back on the agenda. And my heart skipped several beats when he mentioned that two colleges were in the immediate area in Trinidad and Jamaica. By this time, Floyd had made eye contact several times, with a gaze that told me in no uncertain terms that we had to do this. I had no excuse. I had a willing accomplice. One of the two colleges was in a neighboring territory. And with two years of teachers' college under my belt, I was more than halfway toward completing a bachelor's degree. Talk about being in the right place at the right time and with the right person. In church.

Floyd and I converged in an unplanned location when the service was over, and after the prayer of benediction was said. By then, my decision was reversed, and I was ready to take the plunge into the deep waters of higher education after my graduation from teachers' college later in the year, and after I had spent a year of service working for the government of Barbados that had financed my college education for the past two years.

And so ready we were, Floyd and I, to pursue additional education opportunities, that we wasted no time applying for and securing our passports long before we needed them. To make a long story short, I enrolled in West Indies College (Northern Caribbean University) in Jamaica in 1973, graduating three years later with a BA in Education and biology.

Meanwhile, Floyd enrolled in Caribbean Union College (Southern Caribbean University) in Trinidad to work on a degree in Theology. Since then, I had gone on to earn an MA degree, an Ed.S degree, and a doctoral degree in Education (Ed.D), the same one I said I wanted when my tutor at Erdiston Teachers' College had written it on the board not so long ago.

Needless to say, that Saturday in church was an unforgettable day. The events set in motion a series of opportunities that changed my life for the better. I happened to be in the right place at the right time. In church. Not by coincidence or by chance, but simply by respecting the value of church attendance that my parents had instilled so long ago. I am sure they could not foresee my journey or the opportunities opening up when they valued, modeled, and encouraged church attendance. All they wanted when they signed us up was that we attend church and grow into morally cultured children. And church attendance has done just that. And more.

In their simplicity of thought, combined with the absence of exposure to formal education beyond what was basic, they could not imagine that church attendance for me and my siblings could lead to advanced degrees and all that comes with them. For sure, they had never heard of advanced degrees, so their insistence on church attendance was not an ulterior motive on their part. Neither were they privy to research findings that affirmed the values and benefits that are inherent in the practice of regular church attendance: better sleep; less risk of depression and suicide; more stable; longer life; reflection on gratitude; opportunity to give back; and a deeper meaning in one's life. Their only goal was that we attend church and learn to value it as much as they did, remaining unaware of the valuable extras that church-going would make possible.

<u>Extended Value-added Thinking and Actions:</u>

1. Make a list of the positive things church attendance has done for you? What improvements would you love to see in your Church that would make it more appealing to you and the youth of the Church? Share your thoughts with the leadership.

2. Have you ever dropped out of Church? Why? What brought you back?

3. Research findings say that young people leave the church due to the lack of targeted programs; they feel unaccepted; and that church is irrelevant. List some specifics that indicate your agreement or disagreement with the research conclusions.

4. Gather a group of young people from your church and let them talk about the research findings mentioned above and if they have ever experienced those feelings and needs. Entertain their thoughts and ideas as to how they can be satisfied.

Chapter 3
Making Use of Opportunities

Opportunity is missed by most people because it is dressed in overalls and looks like work.

-Thomas Edison

I had no plans to write a chapter focused on opportunities when the idea to write this book was conceived. This is a compilation of values; especially those promoted by my parents and the other residents and parents of Roebuck when my peers and I were growing into young adults; and even before that.

My parents consistently modeled several enviable virtues and values every day and for a long time; two of which I articulated at length in previous chapters. Strangely, they never mentioned the word opportunity as a value that we should emulate, even though as I write, I now see how they created opportunities and held on to some that they copied from other people and sources. Like most in our neighborhood, my parents were simple folk who did not read extensively and were probably not even aware that the word opportunity existed. It was not a word in their limited vocabulary.

My mother never said, "Many opportunities will open up for you if you finish high school." Or my father never said that there would be many opportunities waiting for you if you connect with the right people. Even if they had the word stored in their tool kit, they never pulled it out; choosing to settle for simpler terminology with which they were more comfortable.

Nonetheless, they absolutely knew what an opportunity was, and they grabbed those that were good and perfect for them and our family; some of which may appear simple by today's standards. For example, they welcomed the opportunity to rent a plot of land - a house spot, from the plantation on which to build their own house, and took the opportunity, especially my mother, to join with a number of the local residents to enter in an investment opportunity, commonly known as a *meeting* - an arrangement in which she and other like-minded women contributed a predetermined amount of cash (a hand) each week to the pot, only to collect a lump sum (a turn), also at a predetermined time. Furthermore, she took the opportunity to enhance her *turn* when she learned that she could *throw* multiple hands.

Undoubtedly, the most remembered opportunity is the one my father took advantage of when he migrated to England to seek better opportunities for the family.

I mentioned each of the above just to say that, in retrospect, it was clear that my parents aggressively valued the taking of opportunities, even though it was not recognized back in the day. The only saying from them that I remember that came close to conveying the message that we were to look for opportunities is, "You have to turn out better than me." That was their way of telling us that greater opportunities were out there, waiting for us to grab. In short, they did not want us to grow up toiling in the plantation cane fields in the hot sun or working from sunup to sundown, hoeing weeds from among the corn, yams, and potato plants Monday to Friday. Not that there was anything wrong with the nature of this kind of work, but it had its place, as was discussed in a previous chapter.

"Turn out," they would say. Come to think of it, we would have had to be pretty shortsighted, and even backward had we not been equipped with enough common sense to interpret correctly what 'turn out' meant. It was the local vernacular for opportunities. It was their mantra. And hearing it and seeing how they went after their opportunities, not even for selfish motives but sacrificially, helped to make it possible for us to achieve ours.

So, all along, our parents had been teaching us a lesson that there is value in going after opportunities that may come our way. Although the teaching was not as planned and intentional as the lessons in hard work and church attendance articulated earlier. Their examples were still blatant, aggressive, and overt. So much so that we, and many of our peers, have automatically and seemingly involuntarily become something of an expert at accepting specific opportunities that have dropped in our proverbial laps and, at times, vigorously chasing down others.

I detailed at length one such opportunity in the previous chapter. As mentioned, I happened to be in the right place at the right time. But that was just the beginning. One thing I learned from that experience is that in most instances, opportunities do not always speak your language; they do not always slap you in the face announcing their availability; neither do they always come ready-made. I got this nugget on Messenger from Hal, a good friend. He wrote, "If opportunity doesn't knock, build a door." I think the message is clear and needs no explanation.

Having said all that, my message to youngsters and older ones is simply this. Pay attention. Listen to people. You'll never know what you will hear or what lesson of value you will learn. Develop that habit and perfect it over time. Doing so has the almost unfailing potential to motivate and inspire you to rethink your attitude, create personal possibilities, and even rescind long-held beliefs and decisions.

You will find that there is great value that is inherent in paying close attention to others as they speak. In many cases, it is a safe place that will give birth to the occasional idea or the unexpected opportunity to come flying your way. That's the true nature of opportunities. They are like projectiles looking for a target to strike or a receiver to reach out and gather them in. That receiver can be no better person than you.

And just in case you may be wondering, ideas for opportunities are not sourced only from formal environments like the Church, political speeches and debates, and the halls and lecture rooms of academia. They are conceived and birthed anywhere people talk back and forth with each other. People are always talking, even though they may not be speaking to you directly: at the ball field; at dinner; waiting in line at the grocery store; on the bus or train; and on cell phones in airport terminals; and at the gym, even in public bathrooms everywhere. Go out and check this out for yourself and see if my assertions are valid.

I am not suggesting that you eavesdrop on conversations that are not directed at you, but hearing conversations between third parties is not illegal. Hear as much as you can, especially if what you are hearing is positive, interesting, legal, and rich with ideas for opportunities that you can think seriously of adopting.

Just recently, I was in a conversation with a young lady at church who had not too long ago launched her own marketing business completely online. She is a visionary and talked enthusiastically and passionately about what she does for local and national businesses. It was the perfect conversation for like-minded youngsters to eavesdrop.

You heard me correctly when I wrote that 'stealing' ideas is not a criminal act. I would know firsthand and would have been prosecuted countless times in the past if the act was considered criminal. I am a retired educator, and in my line of work, the *stealing* of ideas is rampant, especially now that the internet is global. Everything from lesson plans to materials, classroom management, administrative ideas, and videos is available for free in many cases. But the richest source I have discovered is listening to teachers talk and reflect on their teaching, and fellow principals and administrators talk freely about their experiences and how they handled them.

In the same way that it is not illegal to listen in on others' public conversations, it is not wrong or immoral to hijack their ideas and use them to your benefit. Besides, people find much pleasure in talking about themselves in public. It feeds the ego, especially if they have risen from nothing to a place of prominence and stature. Listen to your politicians, even when it is disingenuous on your part. They are more than proud to share that they were born in poverty, grew up in the projects and public housing, were the first ones in the family to go to college, "and look at me now."

People are motivated to talk, especially if they have an audience. They love talking about where they went to school; how hard they studied; what degrees they have earned; what they do for a living; how they built a thriving business or a successful career; the research they do; the discoveries they have made; the mistakes they have made; how they built and maintained a successful marriage; how much money they make; how they plant a thriving garden year after year; and the exotic and faraway places they visit around the globe. The more they talk, and the more intentionally you listen, the more likely they will drop at least a morsel of inspiration that you can perhaps begin thinking about seriously.

Just in case you may be wondering why I am so laser-focused on cultivating a habit of listening to others, it is because my parents, especially my mother, appeared to have valued and appreciated it when I was a kid. Come to think of it, my memory serves me correctly. I now clearly recall how she and other women in the neighborhood had the habit of informally gathering in each other's houses from time to time. Now, I firmly believe that these loosely structured gatherings were not gripe sessions about how difficult their lot in life was. Neither were they gossip sessions that focused on belittling and downgrading the character of others in the community. Rather, it is now apparent that these outdated cottage meetings were no more than listening and sharing forums and free seminars that generated ideas and opportunities on how to support one another and improve their standing.

I have little doubt that it was at such assemblies that suggestions, ideas, and information on how to be an active member of the local investment group (commonly known as a meeting) that rewarded members with a large lump sum of cash at one time, which they used to repair a leaky roof, or pay some nagging outstanding bills, or catch up on private school tuition. It is also not beyond the realm of possibility that it was at one of these irregularly called cabin conferences that my mother and others in attendance absorbed vital information, techniques, and strategies in how and when to rotate crops in the plot of land to the east that she rented from Sedgepond Plantation. I can't say for sure that she went out of her way to teach me the value of listening to others, but she was definitely more overt in her attitude, encouragement, and modeling as far as chasing down opportunities was concerned. That's what "you got to turn out better than me" meant.

I said all of that just to make a small but very significant point, especially to young people, or anyone else for that matter, who may be actively looking for a breakthrough; for a chance to break out of the malaise of despair and hopelessness. Listening to others may just be the place to start. It worked for me. If you recall, I listened to a preacher one Saturday while in church, and that one small listening session was the beginning of a series of opportunities that have come my way; some of which I will continue to articulate as the narrative progresses.

But having said all of that about listening to others, let me hasten to add that listening is useless unless it is accompanied by action. Purposeful action, if only mental action at the outset, is an action that is motivated by a series of unspoken belief statements. This is what sets one apart from the casual listener. As you listen to others, you must simultaneously say to yourself, "I want that." Or "I can do that." Or "if she can do that, I can do it also." "If he can make that, I can make one as well." I am writing this from personal experience. This is a phenomenon that actually happened to me.

While listening to the preacher talk about education, I kept self-motivating for close to an hour. I had never spoken to myself like this before, but it felt good and liberating when I kept forcing myself to silently say "I can do this. I can go back to school." I was well aware that challenges were sure to be a part of the experience, but I would deal with those at the appropriate time.

Now was the time for me to motivate myself. When this happens, you are telling yourself that you are just as talented and just as creative, and what is more important, you are affirming that you believe in yourself, which must happen before others begin to believe in you. You become your personal cheerleading section. A cheerleading team of one. A planning committee of one.

In my personal journey, I took action almost immediately after listening to that Saturday morning preacher at church. I, along with my friend, Floyd, wasted no time in applying for a passport. Truth be told, we took this action even before we knew when we would need the document, or to which far-away land we would be flying. When you take such drastic and immediate steps, you confirm your own personal seriousness, as well as build a starting place and a foundation on which to construct your way forward.

Such early steps provide a wealth of motivation and are the source of intense focus, purpose, and direction. When I picked up my passport, as insignificant as the event may have seemed to others, it had a way of confirming that this boy was going somewhere, that there was no turning back now. How could I disappoint my passport by refusing to act to embrace the opportunity that was beginning to open up for me?

So, if you listen to executives, business tycoons, farmers, teachers, carpenters, and even preachers, you may come away with an idea that you can turn into an opportunity; the idea that you can turn your kitchen table hamburger recipe into a thriving hamburger joint. Just don't call it McDonald's. Or that you can perfect a mixture of Clorox bleach and dish-washing liquid into an all-purpose cleaner. Just don't call your invention 409. On a serious note, the lesson I am trying to teach is that listening to others can produce a treasure trove of ideas. It is a skill to be developed and practiced, especially if you are on the lookout for strategies and concepts to enrich your life.

I have come to realize that listening to others, in many ways, can be a personal learning experience in more ways than one. For one, you may come to discover that others may be more aware of your talents, abilities, and potential than you are. A case in point. When I was a young teacher at All Saints Boys School, my principal, Mr. Vaughn approached me with a question that stunned me for a brief moment. "When are you going to college," he inquired. I was somewhat taken aback because of the way in which he posed the question. "When are you going to college?" Not, "Are you planning on going to college?" Apparently, he had seen something in me that I had not seen in myself. That was motivation enough to inspire me to seek out the possible opportunities that were fundamental in pursuing a college education.

Such may have been the case with the following story that I heard on NPR's *How I Built This* some time ago. Jerry Murrell, founder of *Five Guys Burgers and Fries,* told the story of how he and his wife had built a simple burger that turned out to be very tasty and just as popular with their customers at the small takeout restaurant they opened. The outfit did so well that Jerry decided to leave his full-time job. He was quite comfortable in managing a single operation and had a feeling of satisfaction and security running one business. That was enough. That was until his sons suggested the franchise opportunity. It took some convincing, but he eventually relented and went along with their recommendation. By 2012, the chain had stores in over a thousand locations operating in over forty-seven states and Canada.

As I listened to the story, I did not hear a single mention of regret; only mention of accomplishments, success, growth, expansion, and gratefulness for listening to others, and for taking the risks that the opportunity presented. I am sure that there are numerous what-if questions that are often asked by Jerry. "What if I had not listened to the idea of franchising? What if I had not embraced the opportunity when I did? What if I had not taken advantage of the spin-off opportunities that are byproducts (by-opportunities) of many initial opportunities?"

A little later, a second story on How I Built This caught my attention. I am interjecting it into the narrative at this point for three main reasons. One is because of the spin-off opportunities that resulted, and also because the main character in the story is not only a woman, but a black woman: two factors relative to gender and race that are often cited as barriers to opportunities for minority women.

Janice Bryant Howroyd tells the story of how she managed to create the staffing agency, The ActOne Group. According to Janice, she had moved to California to visit her sister, and went to work for her brother-in-law. In her own words, she "worked magic in the office." When he returned from a business trip, he was so impressed with her organizational and management skills that he encouraged her to start her own business. Today, The ActOne Group is one of the largest staffing groups in the world, generating an average of one billion dollars in net sales. Janice is one of the richest self-made women in America, and according to Forbes, she has amassed a personal fortune of 420 million dollars.

This story, as well as the one cited above, makes clearer the observation I have been trying to make – the fact that others may see the potential, the skills, and the talent in us that we do not see in ourselves, and the reason they mention their observations to us is to make us aware that there are opportunities out there for us to pursue. Many times, we take it lightly when we are commended for our unconscious and natural display of common sense, creativity, intelligence, and superior thinking, choosing rather to doubt, or even disregard the sentiments that are thrown in our direction.

When this happens, we close the door to learning more about ourselves and what makes us unique, and may even throw away forever any and every chance of parlaying our aptitudes, gifts, and capabilities into opportunities that could benefit us personally, as well as our community and the larger society.

That's why whenever I am complimented for some performance, be it teaching a college class, providing professional advice to a colleague, or for doing something as simple as keeping my lawn neat and manicured, I wholeheartedly believe the sentiments expressed, taking the compliments seriously and thankfully. After all, what kind of person would waste precious time and breath to communicate false and misleading thoughts? The fact remains that there is a personal uniqueness and a bank of endowments in each of us that can be turned into special and successful prospects and opportunities.

On the other hand, you may be surprised to learn that other people, friends, classmates, and even strangers, may even find it interesting listening to you. In other words, you too can be an unlikely source of information and encouragement to others, even though you may not think of yourself as smart enough, resourceful enough, or sufficiently experienced in one or more disciplines or fields of study. Similarly, you may not think of yourself as possessing an adequate level of experiential knowledge and expertise that you have amassed by simply engaging in work, experimentation or personal study.

I had such an experience in the gym one evening. I had not met Kyle before, but he was interested in my workout routine because of the way I moved from one machine or activity to the next without taking much of a break. My explanation was that I do not see the need for cardio when I work out like this. He found the information useful and said he would follow my example because it made sense to him, even though the tips I passed on were not gained from a fitness expert or from a professional with expertise in this domain. As we talked he was surprised at my age and wanted to know what I ate and what I did for a living. I shared that I was into plant-based dieting, drinking lots of water, and cutting out sugar from my diet as much as possible.

Kyle was nineteen and shared that he wanted to get into technology and writing. He perked up when I told him that I had published two books and was working on two more. He was struggling with the basics of writing and did not know how and where to begin. "Just start writing," I instructed. "Write every day and keep a pen and paper with you during the day and by your bedside at night because ideas pop up at odd moments. And don't worry about editing. That will come later." He was grateful for my advice and thanked me heartily.

My point is that you too are blessed with knowledge, expertise, and experience that you can dispense to those who are opportunity seekers. I ended the conversation with Kyle with the following nugget of advice because he repeated that he was nineteen and the years were passing by quickly. "Don't count the years. Make the years count for you," I told him. I thought it was too deep, profound, and impressive a sentiment to have originated with me, so I went home and googled the expression and discovered that one George Meredith had said something similar: "Don't just count your years. Make your years count." In either case, it is good and timely advice.

It was mentioned earlier that my mother and the other senior residents of my neighborhood appeared to have relished the opportunity to jump at every chance to improve their lot in life, as well as that of their families. Although they used extreme caution and careful attention concerning the talk of new opportunities that were popular, they did not adopt a 'do it tomorrow attitude' that had as its basic premise, delaying and putting off for another day. On the contrary, their thinking and attitude were more in line with the ancient proverb that advises all to make hay while the sun shines.

It was this attitude that motivated them to join a *meeting*, a local organization run by a group of residents, where each member invested a set amount of money in a pool each week and collected a lump sum when it was their turn. They saw this as an opportunity to cash in on a substantial amount of money, which they used to pay bills, repair the house, and raise their standard of living.

I wrote about this opportunity and investment strategy in some detail in my 2010 book, *It's Your Word Against Mine,* and pointed out that even though the organization was loosely run without elected officials to serve as president, vice president, secretary, accountant, or treasurer; or without the use of financial houses such as banks and credit unions to store the collected cash; or without the creation of a business plan, bylaws or tax plans, the local residents saw this as an opportunity, and invited participation based solely on trust, hearty relationships, and a corporate desire to get ahead.

Large amounts of cash changed hands in weekly transactions in this opportunity arrangement, but what is more remarkable is the fact that in all my years of watching and studying this opportunity, I am unable to recall even one incident of stealing, misappropriation of funds, inability to pay out, or money laundering. However, chasing after such opportunities is risky business that is fraught with uncertainty, anxiety, and fear. Still, they repeated their business agreement time and time again and reaped the benefits and rewards the opportunity had to offer.

But they did not stop there. They chased down other opportunities. It became their way of life, giving the impression that they adored the challenge of at least trying, just to see how the challenges would work out, and what other opportunities they would eventually pursue. Times were hard. Good jobs that paid enough to adequately support growing families were not plentiful.

And because the conditions were what they were at the time, those thoughtful women and family-oriented men, sought opportunities elsewhere - across the seas. The harsh conditions no doubt challenged their basic belief and manly perceptions that it was up to real men to care for their families and provide for their financial, physical, and emotional well being.

So, they sought opportunities across the seas. To England, to be specific. My own father, along with his brother, Hattan, and others like my cousin, Hugh, and Coursey, not only thought about the opportunity, but took the bull by the horn, as the saying goes. They said goodbye to their families, and migrated to England in hot pursuit of opportunities they hoped would make life easier for themselves and their families back home.

But as mentioned previously, challenges, anxiety, and fear are all notable prerequisites one needs to conquer while on the rugged journey to the opportunity zone. These seemingly ubiquitous deterrents automatically present themselves without invitation at practically every human adventure. But be that as it may, my parents and their cohorts were able to prove that the human competitive spirit, coupled with an attitude of fierce determination, are forces that could outlast even the most ferocious attacks that manifested themselves as weapons of fear, self-doubt, and hopelessness.

They believed that an abundance of caution was necessary in their pursuit of worthwhile opportunities. But they also realized that there would come a time when caution, thrown to the wind, was the best way forward. They were fearful, yet determined, and remained fully aware that both fear and determination could coexist in the same body, while being cognizant of the fact   that one of them had to emerge as the dominant force to mask and subdue the recessive. And so, they set sail for a new and faraway land, cautious but optimistic, sacrificing the limited cash they had mustered, in an insecure and risky gamble bombarded by doubt, yet positive and hopeful.

They were ever mindful that failure was an option. So too was success. The value they placed on pursuing opportunities was so strong that they were willing to risk every hard-earned dollar and life and limb in pursuit of every prospect that they thought was worth it.

And so, they doggedly persevered, complaining as they progressed. The voyage by sea was too long. The English weather was unkind and unwelcoming. The struggle to adjust to a new culture was real. And the pursuit of job opportunities was tough. But they did it. And the rest is history. As I write this, a quote by Dr. Juliet Daniel, a professor at McMaster University, is note-worthy. She eloquently stated, "You have to move out of your comfort zone to reach your full potential." And that's exactly what those brave men from Roebuck did when they decided to migrate to the UK in search of opportunities.

Happily, those lessons and examples of scouting out opportunities did not go unnoticed, or fall on deaf ears, even if only unconsciously. Later my siblings and others from our small community successfully pursued their own educational and professional opportunities in the US, England, and Canada. I have already mentioned how I capitalized on an opportunity to continue my education in Jamaica after learning of the opportunity in church that Saturday morning. Still, there was one more time when I grabbed hold of another opportunity; one that would pay dividends years down the road.

Prior to providing details on that specific journey, I sincerely hope that those of you reading this have already learned, discovered, or affirmed, that the special characteristic associated with opportunity-seeking is that success in one opportunity opens the door to one, two, or even more. Opportunity-seeking is not static by nature. It is a dynamic process that can inevitably lead to limitless others for those that decide to seriously pursue the undertaking.

Here is my story, as promised. I graduated with a Masters degree from Andrews University in Berrien Springs on August 9, 1981. My wife Hortense and I already had a two-year-old son, and as luck would have it, our second was born later that celebratory evening. The prearranged plans called for Hortense to matriculate at Michigan State University in East Lansing the upcoming fall semester in September, to begin work towards her Masters. Her classes were in the evening, so she was at home during the day with the boys, while I worked with a team, cleaning student housing in Spartan Village.

As mentioned in a previous chapter, the nature of this kind of work did not deter me. The work of buffing floors, dusting, scrubbing walls, cleaning toilets, and replacing ceiling tiles, even though it was laborious, was predated by work that was just as punishing: cleaning pig pens and chicken coops, hauling dung, and caring for a flock of stubborn sheep. The completion of those manual prerequisites that I mastered in my youth came in handy at this time. At the same time, it was honorable and purposeful work that contributed to the economy of our home, a concept that was developed in a previous chapter.

But the schedule mentioned above freed up time for me to sacrifice what little time I had available to seek other opportunities to continue my education by working on an additional graduate degree. I was home from work by noon to help look after the boys, while Hortense studied in the library, worked on assignments, or prepared for her evening classes two or three days a week. That left two or three days a week for me to enroll in classes, especially those starting rather late, when she was either not attending scheduled classes, or was sometimes just getting out of class.

We made the schedule work so that the opportunities that were there for the taking, were pursued. By the time Hortense graduated in the spring of 1982, I had only two more classes left to finish my Ed.S (Educational Specialist) degree, and would have taken one of them, had we not been busy packing up to move back to St. Croix in the Virgin Islands to pursue teaching opportunities. I took one of the required classes in the evenings after school at the College of the Virgin Islands, and returned to Michigan State the following summer to take that one class that was required.

The point that I am trying to make is simple: opportunities are there for the taking, and only the wise, the ambitious, the alert, and the attentive, will put themselves in a frame of mind to position themselves to capitalize on them when they become available; at times not simply waiting for them to emerge, but actively making them happen for you, especially when one is almost positive that a particular opportunity may never present itself again. And that was my thinking at the time.

When would I ever be in a similar situation again? Why not take hold of the present and what it offered, not knowing what the future would promise? Or would not promise. And what made the opportunity so much sweeter was the fact that compared to tuition and other costs at Andrews University, Michigan State was more affordable, especially when minority grants, Equal Opportunity grants, and the like, were factored in; so much so that I graduated owing nothing to Michigan State, or to a student loan organization.

Please pardon me if I have misled anyone into believing that the above-mentioned situation was as simple and uncomplicated as I might have described it. The truth is that it was quite the opposite. Hortense and I have often reminisced, with a fair amount of humor and satisfaction, concerning some of the things we did to make this opportunity work for us.

I remember waiting and looking out the apartment door for the appearance of the bus which would bring her home from class on those frigid, dark days of a Michigan winter. As the bus approached the bus stop, I would dash out the door, our paths intersecting as we slipped and balanced ourselves on the icy terrain. I was off to class, and she made it home just in time to relieve me of my babysitting duties.

Secondly, the experience took almost every ounce of physical conditioning I had. After enduring the nature of the work I did in the mornings, I had to dig deep for that extra drop of strength to remain alert and attentive in the 6:00 pm to 9: 00 pm classes. And please don't bother asking where we found the time to study, write term papers, and satisfy other class requirements while being full-time parents to two infant boys. The truth is that we hired a teenage babysitter to look after them when our schedules got too hectic. We did what we had to do to make the opportunities work for us.

I still laugh to myself when I revisit those days in my mind. One particular memory stands out. One day I was riding past our apartment on the van that transported us between jobs in the expansive Spartan Village complex. Suddenly, the apartment door flew open, and I was just in time to witness our older son escape in a quick run down the sidewalk with Denise, our babysitter, in hot pursuit. The sight of my young son bolting and being chased was funny, but not for one moment did I feel guilty for leaving our young ones in the care of someone else while I pursued an opportunity that I was sure would never come my way again. I was not sacrificing my children's security or jeopardizing their development in any way. If I felt that way, another option would have been used.

I wrote what I just said to solidify a point I articulated earlier - that opportunities are just what they appear to be on the surface - just an opportunity. But going after an opportunity is another story that takes work, personal sacrifice, and a willingness to restructure one's thinking, one's attitude, one's priorities, and last but not least, one's schedule and one's time.

Similarly, the journey into opportunity land also begins with competing choices -the choice to go for it, or the choice to do nothing, or with competing excuses such as the following: I can't do it because I am from a poor family; I am not educated enough; I have failed so many times before; I don't want to take the chance, or suppose I lose everything.

So, if you find yourself fighting with these and other competing choices and excuses, you are not in a place that has never been trodden before. Be advised that the world's great and famous thinkers, inventors, educators, artists, and parents, occupied that space a long time before you have. Even my parents and others like them were there at one time or another. What if they had remained there? I was there. I am so thrilled that I decided to take that first step.

But my parents were far from the only ones to value taking or seeking opportunities. They were in good company in this aspect. I woke up on Easter morning a while back, just at the right time to catch an interview Willie Geist was having with the great basketball superstar, Shaquelle O'Neal. I didn't know, or may have forgotten, that Shaq had tried his hand at acting, and had even starred in one or two movies, the names of which elude me. But Shaq was quick to mention that one of the movies in which he had starred had the distinction of being the 'best worst movie.' And then Willie asked this follow-up, "Do you think your dabbling in acting posed a threat to your NBA career?" Shaq quietly replied, "We must take advantage of all opportunities."

All opportunities? I mulled that statement over in my mind for a while, with the obvious question forming the basis for my mental exploration. How can anyone take advantage of all opportunities, as Shaq so eloquently asserted? Is it really possible? And is it as easy as he made it appear to be? My conclusion is that his assertion has some merit, that all opportunities that come our way deserve some serious attention, even though they may be pulling us in a completely different direction from the one that was originally intended.

Shaq's statement also led to some serious personal reflection and introspection that gave rise to even more questions. How many opportunities had I squandered in the past? Will I be more attentive and open to opportunities that will come my way in the future? Had I taken advantage of any specific opportunities that showed up in my past and capitalized on them to the extent that I have reaped the benefits? Or am I still enjoying present-day benefits, even though my actions on those opportunities are long gone? And finally, have those opportunities led to others down the road? There is a mixed bag of responses; some in the affirmative, and others not. However, there was one opportunity that I went after with much enthusiasm, even though kicking and screaming in the initial stages.

I have previously discussed the events that led up to my going to Jamaica to work on a college degree back in the seventies, 1973-1976, to be exact. And I have also mentioned how some opportunities just show up out of the blue; some may emerge from simply listening to peoples' conversations that may or may not be deliberately directed at you. And I have also affirmed that opportunities do not always jump up and slap you in the face. I have personal experience with an opportunity that can fit snugly into two of the categories I just listed. It showed up out of the blue and was quite a surprise. Even to this day, I still reminisce about the events of that day..

It was June of 1976, and I had just completed my secondary education degree with a Biology major at West Indies College (now Northern Caribbean University) in Jamaica. I was alone in my room since my roommates, all Jamaican nationals, had already said their goodbyes. My suitcase was packed, and I was lying on my bare mattress for the last time, contemplating my ride to the airport to catch my flight back to Barbados in a day or two. I was ready and excited to be finally going back home for the first time in three long years when Mr. Opportunity came calling.

The student attendant managing the desk in the lobby announced over the public address system that there was an overseas telephone call for me. Surprised, I scurried down the four flights of stairs to take the call from a gentleman I had never met or even heard of. "This is Pastor Carneigie from The North Caribbean Conference of Seventh-day Adventists in St. Croix. How are you?" He continued, "I understand that you have just graduated with a degree in Biology, and I am extending a call to you to teach at our school in St. Croix. We are looking for a science teacher." I was somewhere between shock and surprise and did not think to ask him how he had heard about me or how or when I would interview. But I remember becoming very defensive and began to explain why I could not go to St. Croix. "But I am going back to Barbados tomorrow," I countered. "Why not take a couple of hours to think and pray about my offer, and I will call you back?"

You should know that very early in my youth, I had made an unannounced and personal promise to myself that I would never leave Barbados. Although I had not traveled much outside the country or was exposed to the life and culture of other places, I was absolutely sure that life in Barbados was the best. And it was.

In the sixties and seventies, the economy in Barbados was good, crime was relatively non-existent, jobs were available, education was a priority and superior, and the political system was strong and viable. I enjoyed growing up in Barbados and had no reason or motivation to leave. And even if I did leave, I would be gone only for a brief time and come right back, as is the case with me going to Jamaica. In all honesty I must admit that I fell in love with Jamaica because of the common similarities to Barbados. And to say that I enjoyed my experience on campus is an understatement. Still, I was determined and adamant about returning home.

Secondly, when I went to Jamaica, apart from my determination to return to Barbados after my studies, I was absolutely sure that this would be the end of my formal education; that I had had enough schooling; that I had already achieved way beyond my expectations, and the expectations others had for me. I was done. I was not willing to proceed further, even though I was more than confident that I possessed the academic talent and ability to successfully handle the academic rigor that is expected at the graduate level of education.

Strangely enough, I interacted with fellow students who had visions of pursuing educational opportunities beyond the undergraduate level, and with faculty and professors that had earned masters and doctoral degrees. Just being immersed in the richness and stimulation of the academic environment, my initial decision began to decline little by little. By the end of three years, I had already entertained thoughts about returning to school. Not just to any school. But to Andrews University in Berrien Springs, Michigan, the premier Seventh-day Adventist institution that was talked about and promoted highly on campus. And right along with those thoughts were the obvious questions and concerns. First, I don't have a US visa. And most importantly, I don't have the US dollars to finance such a venture.

So, what does all of this have to do with the call from Pastor Carneigie and the opportunity he was inviting me to consider? If you can recall, I mentioned earlier that the journey into opportunity land begins with competing choices and competing excuses. That was exactly where I found myself when I got the call from St. Croix. I walked back upstairs towards my room, intending to pray about the opportunity as the Pastor had recommended. However, by the time I reached Room 410, I had already decided to accept the invitation and the opportunity to teach in St. Croix. And to be fully transparent and honest, I did not pray about it as was suggested by the Pastor because somewhere between the first floor and the fourth floor of the men's dorm, I weighed the competing excuses and the competing choices and made a decision.

The key factor in my decision-making was that it would be much easier to save US dollars to finance a graduate degree if I worked in St. Croix and received US currency. Secondly, I had no job offer in Barbados, and here I was, being offered a job and an opportunity, even without an interview, found myself making all kinds of excuses about wanting to return to Barbados because I loved the place so much.

Pastor Carnegie called back as promised, and he was delighted that I had a change of heart, and the opportunity was sealed. "Go on to Barbados," he instructed, "and wait for your visa from the US embassy. At least you get to go back to Barbados," he humored me. I went back to Barbados andpicked up my H1 visa later in the summer of 1976, a visa thatwas "highly desired by so many" according to the consul (Constance Huggins; I even remember her name).

It was tough leaving Barbados, but somehow I entertained the thought that once I got on that BWIA jet for a short layover in Puerto Rico before landing in St. Croix, that it would be either the last time or a very long time before I would be back in Barbados, or that I may never live there again permanently. Nevertheless, an opportunity had opened up for me, and I grabbed it, even though it meant giving up on some long-held promises.

To make a long story short, I went to St. Croix and did the best teaching I have ever done. The opportunity put me in partnership with a wonderful staff and a bunch of students that were very aggressive in learning, studying, and who were very career-oriented. Many now hold positions of responsibility and leadership in various fields: medicine, business, education, nursing, etc. I remain grateful for the opportunity to serve in that capacity. I was simply following the example of my parents as they aggressively modeled how to go after opportunities that came their way.

But that's just the thing that opportunity-seeking does to the fervent seeker. It can force one on a track that they would not normally take. Apart from that, it drives us out of our comfort zone of ease and satisfaction into the sphere of discomfort to seek new, difficult, and uncertain challenges. Simply speaking, opportunity-seeking is not for the faint of heart, the timid, the fearful, or those of a cowardly disposition. Rather the seeker of opportunities is adventurous, assertive, and unafraid.

These are the very attributes my mother and those like her possessed when they invested their hard-earned cash ina loosely organized scheme, simply called a *meeting*. It is a certainty that they were confronted with the competing choices and excuses I mentioned earlier. And it is also indisputable that the usual questions were the source of concern and apprehension: What if I lose everything? What if other investors, for one reason or another, fail to keep their end of the bargain? And the most concerning, will I be able to recoup some or all of my investment?

Still, they chose to be positive, ambitious, and aspiring, with a chance at entrepreneurship and a better life for themselves and their families.

Take a brief moment and reflect on one or more adventures you have taken, thought about taking, or are presently thinking about undertaking. Whether it is writing a book, going back to school, dating him or her, running a marathon, or taking up violin lessons. If you are honest and transparent, you will, without hesitation, confess that one or more of the competing choices, questions, and concerns mentioned previously, presented themselves very early in your thinking: I am not a good writer. Nobody would be interested in reading what I write. I am too old. I am not good at chemistry. Others will make fun of me. What if I fail? And the list goes on and on. How did you confront those demons? What was the result? And best of all, what were the *by-opportunities* that spun off from your adventure?

By now, it should no longer be a secret that my parents placed a high value on risk-taking and seeking out opportunities. Whether it was my father's risky decision to migrate to England to find work opportunities or my mother's venture into the many opportunity-seeking undertakings. I was surprised at her spunk as she ventured into the arena of trying something new just to find ways to improve our standard of living.

Whether it was the investment *meeting* adventure, or her efforts to acquire a plot of land from the plantation on which to build our own home, or her push to encourage each of us to pursue our own risks and opportunities as far as education was concerned, it now appears that she may have been more excited at the prospects of the spun-off opportunities than the initial startup ventures themselves. As a result, she could now do good on her plan to send me to a private school, repair a leaking roof, and could more fully enjoy the pleasure of home ownership.

So, I grew up privy to my mother's value and high regard for going after those opportunities that she thought would provide a better living for us and the risks associated with them, plus the secondary opportunities that sprung from the original. But that was her experience. Not mine, even though I believed she was teaching by example and hoping that value would somehow be transferred to my siblings and me.

Earlier, I elaborated on my experience of going to St. Croix to teach instead of returning to Barbados. I also referred to the conclusion that the opportunity turned into the best teaching of my career. That being the case, some of you may be wondering if there were any secondary opportunities that spun off from the initial one. I am delighted to report that they were some. One in particular.

You are already aware that one of the reasons that informed my decision to go to St. Croix was my eagerness and ability to fund my graduate education on the mainland. I felt that working in the US territory and receiving a salary in US dollars would make the opportunity easier. That opportunity did show up in a strange and unexpected fashion, one that left me stunned and still boggles my mind, and continues to give rise to numerous questions to this day.

One morning, about a year after I arrived on the island, I had just finished teaching a tenth-grade Biology class when my principal, Mr. Griffin, bounded into the classroom with his usual high-octane level of excitement and enthusiasm. "You have to go down to the embassy as soon as possible. They are giving away green cards to science and math teachers," he encouraged. I did as instructed and started the process, filled in the required papers, secured the requested documents, took and passed a physical, and had my green card in hand shortly thereafter.

I had not saved much money to this point, but I was armed with a green card that paved the way and provided those opportunities to which I was now entitled as a legal US resident.

Later I enrolled in Andrews University as a graduate student, graduating in 1981 with a Master's degree, an event and experience that was the precursor to even more personal and professional opportunities down the road.

The questions and what-ifs surrounding how this opportunity opened up for me are numerous and varied. Questions I roll over in my mind every now and then, especially when I feel grateful, thankful, and even lucky. Why me? Suppose I had not studied science in college, but had decided to major in History, English, or some other discipline. Would this opportunity have opened up in another way? What if I had not decided to pursue the opportunity in St. Croix? I certainly do not know the answer to these questions. Neither am I interested. The important thing to consider is the decision I made when the opportunity presented itself.

One thing I know is that opportunity-seeking has transformed me into a new person; a being that I was unaware of living inside me. It has also taught me that fear and uncertainty of the unknown are motivating factors that propelled me towards a goal and a dream, and that, in many cases, I had to muster the bravery and courage to step out on my own. For example, I went to Jamaica alone, even though I was fed stories of it not being a good idea. And what made my adventure more precarious, was the unknown. I did not know anyone in all of Jamaica. And even more daunting was the supposition and possibility that I might be the only student from Barbados on that campus. (When I got there, I realized that I was the only one, but four more would join me the following year).

Still, I forged ahead with confidence and determination, and with the same gusto and fervor that my mother modeled when she charged headlong, attacking the opportunities that came her way. After all, what use is an opportunity if it is not accompanied by uncertainty and challenge, she must have mused.

And the same is true of my St. Croix experience. I did not know of any Bajans (Barbadians) living there except for Barbara, whom I had only met briefly when I was home that summer before going to St. Croix. She was teaching at the same school where I would be teaching and was home on vacation that summer. Randy, one of the Bajan students that joined me in Jamaica, preceded me to St. Croix by only a few months. Sammy would join us a year or so later. But I went anyway. And look at the good fortune that has attended me, which I continue to enjoy to this day. At the same time, I am not without feelings of guilt and remorse as I, from time to time, reflect on my initial inability and refusal to perceive the richness of the opportunity that was initially offered. Often, I seek forgiveness for my short-sightedness and tunnel vision attitude in wanting to return to Barbados while being hit in the face with a pretty explosive opportunity. My initial fear of the risks involved, and the perceived challenges of the unknown were at work to sideline the opportunity, even before I took the first step.

But that's the very thing that opportunity-seeking is designed to do. My parents knew that. That's why they did what they did and embarked on the risks they took, all in the name of opportunities. They valued it so much that they allowed it to take them where they had never gone before, and to take steps and chances that challenged who they were.

And without a doubt, they passed that value on to us. No wonder we also allowed it to be the force that urged my siblings and me to follow their example. We were willing to risk separation from family, friends, church members, and those who were not as bold, optimistic, and ambitious. It functions as a character-building tool that tests one's faith, surfaces one's strengths and weaknesses, builds patience, encourages learning, boosts self-awareness, and brings to light the stuff you are made of – the stuff that makes you you, and that makes me who I am.

<u>Extended Value-added Thinking and Actions:</u>

1. Take the time to list the skills, talents, and attributes you think you have or those that have earned you compliments from others.

2. Prioritize them and beside each one, write your plans for the steps you are willing to take to strengthen and improve them. Research the opportunities (financial, educational, etc.) that may result from each.

3. Think of one or two persons that you have observed and have concluded that they have made the most of specific opportunities that came their way. What specific qualities did you see? Do you think that you possess those qualities? Make a list of questions you may want to include in an interview or conversation with that person (s) to learn the special characteristics necessary for success.

4. What are some specific opportunities on which you have capitalized? What was the major or initial opportunity? What spin-off opportunities (by-opportunities) resulted? What would you do differently, should you decide to pursue a similar one in the future, or a new one that may come your way?

Chapter 4
Go to School (and learn)

The whole purpose of education is to turn mirrors into windows.

-Sydney J. Harris

When you read the introduction to this work, the hope is that your biggest takeaway from that section is the unmistakable value that was placed on education and schooling by my parents and the other authority figures when we were growing up in Roebuck and the other adjacent districts. Like the values of church attendance and work that were discussed in previous chapters, school attendance was not optional. Unlike church attendance and work, school attendance was the law. We had to go to school, and our parents were the chief enforcers of the schooling statute. Not the government. Our parents were the real enforcement and truant officers. And they took the responsibility seriously, ruling with an iron hand as if they were on the government payroll.

Maybe, just maybe, we could have gotten away with "I don't feel like going to Sunday school today." By the way, this didn't happen. Or our parents would let it slide if the pig pen wasn't cleaned as scheduled. Or the yard wasn't weeded on the date specified. Or the pigeon peas weren't picked on time. But school attendance was not a topic for discussion or a matter to be negotiated. It happened automatically and involuntarily. It was like breathing, heart beating, and swallowing. We simply had to do it. And we did. And we loved it. And that made it very easy for our parents to enforce. I cannot remember ever saying that I didn't like school or that I didn't want to go. It wouldn't have mattered anyway because the school attendance police lived in our house, and they were always on duty.

I distinctly remember going home for lunch from school one day with Yvonne, one of my younger sisters, and after we got home, it rained so heavily and for a long time, so much so that going back to school was threatened. I remember us crying our hearts out because we could not return to school. That's how much we loved school, and it was a testament that the value my parents placed on our schooling was being appreciated.

It is worth repeating that my parents did not have a high school education. I know that they went to primary school, and could handle the basics of reading and writing, and could communicate verbally and ably. But beyond that, their level of education and academic achievement was limited. Their situation was not unlike that of their neighbors, friends, and other family members. A similar educational level of academic achievement was pervasive in the Roebuck neighborhood. And in Indian Ground. And Four Hill.

If research was conducted into the academic standing and level of achievement among my parents' contemporaries, the findings would have been conclusive – that one hundred percent of the study population did not advance beyond the primary level of education. A scientific study was not necessary for one to arrive at this conclusion. A mere observation of the family tree of each adult residing in the small agricultural district would tell the story that neither their parents, grandparents, nor great-grandparents feared any differently from my parents' situation.

Nevertheless, I have always assured myself that had the opportunities been available as they were for me, my parents would have jumped headfirst at the chance to climb to a more advanced level of education. But they enjoyed a sense of security, knowing that they did not have to compete with others, and that there was no need to feel insecure and less than others, for the entire community of residents was occupying the same level.

I was never that bold to inquire of my mother as to the reasons she did not advance beyond the level of education she occupied. However, many theories had crossed my mind, especially when I was able to clearly see how important education was to her, and when I came to realize and understand the enormous value she placed on it; and then to witness first-hand the unselfish and massive effort she expended on our behalf as far as getting an education was concerned.

Just in case I had mustered up the courage to ask, I might have listened intently as she listed the following reasons: no one in my family had gone to high school; I did not have a mentor; none of my friends had gone to high school; I had to work to help support the family. And the list might have gone on and on.

Notice that I did not mention not being smart enough as a reason for my mother's lack of a higher education experience. I am positive that had the opportunities been available, she would have put them to work for her, just like she did with everything else. She was smart, creative, and ambitious enough to handle the rigors and expectations of higher-level education. And the same is true for many others in her circle of friends, companions, and contemporaries in Roebuck.

While we are on the subject of education and achievement, I think it wise to interject the concept of education that was my mother's and the others like her; a concept to which I alluded earlier. The current thinking as it relates to an educated person is diametrically opposed to the view held by my parents when my siblings and I were growing up. In today's parlance, an educated person is characterized in much more glowing terms when compared to my parents' estimation. Terms like bachelor's degree, master's degree, and the like, are commonplace.

Obviously, primary education for us was a must, and they were adamant about that. But to them, the ultimate in education was a successful completion of high school. This supreme goal was rooted in their belief concerning the purpose of education in Barbados. To be fair, they never articulated their thinking out loud, but it is fair to say that they were staunch believers in the notion that the purpose of a high school education was the preparation of students to enter the workforce of the country as teachers, nurses, bank and postal employees, and in the other branches of the civil service. To them, that was the dominant purpose of education for the country and for us as well.

That's exactly where their value on education resided, and that's where their goal to make it a reality for us began. In all fairness, my mother's value of education and her desire to see us obtain it actually began with her. It goes without saying that her implicit and unspoken, yet determined quest, was to arrest the cycle of the undereducated that was permanent and historic among her grandparents, parents, siblings, and the other members of her family and the neighborhood. She must have mused that it was a generational situation and that she was determined to end the cycle. It had to stop. And who better to be tasked with the responsibility than she and the other like-minded parents in Roebuck, even as uneducated and unqualified as they were?

And yet, that value, which she and the others respected and promoted so overtly, must have come at a cost to them. A price not associated with money or financial currency, but a high cost, nonetheless. In my previous book, *It's Your Word Against Mine,* I addressed this subject briefly, but I think it bears repeating here in this context. It must have been a battle to continue promoting education as a value and a necessity with so much effort and enthusiasm when they were acutely aware of their own shortcomings and a lack of a personal track record in this area.

Several questions must have my mother's passion and zeal. Why am I so passionate about something so foreign to me? How can I place so much value on an entity that I have not personally experienced? What makes me qualified to make higher level education attractive and compelling to my children, even though I am not a graduate of an education program beyond the primary level? What right and audacity do I have to insist on, and enforce a program of studies to which I am not capable of contributing?

But the ever-ubiquitous mantra, you have to turn out better than me, must have overshadowed every question she had concerning her own deficiencies as far as her formal education track record was concerned. It was her motto. Her platform. Her manifesto. And so, she went to work with a resolute determination, undeterred at making sure that the value she placed on education was visible to us.

To my mother and her cohorts, the entire venture was an experiment. They provided the laboratory. We were the specimens, whether we were willing or had to be drafted by force. Their primary goal was to make sure that we had a seat on the school bus to high school when it rolled through bright and early at 7:15 every morning. And several of us were on board, even if we had to run half-dressed, like me, to the bus stop some mornings to be there on time for the arriving bus.

But there was an ulterior motive at work. A vicarious and personal achievement that they hoped would bring some measure of inner, and even exterior satisfaction. They were aware of the positives that their value on education would have on us, the recipients. But what was in it for them? What visible personal benefits and levels of gratification would be their reward after investing an enormous amount of persuasive, economic, and prayerful capital on our behalf?

One thing is for sure. They were not interested in recouping the vast amount of dollars they invested on our behalf. That thought was never given a resting place in their minds. It was never sown there, so it could not germinate and mature to bear selfish fruit. They had more lofty thoughts that would be the basis for their expected rewards. Rewards that were intangible. But just as valuable.

I mentioned in *It's Your Word Against Mine* the degree of pride and satisfaction I observed on my mother's face when I stepped out of the house dressed in my shirt and tie that first morning I reported as a teacher at All Saints Boys School. It is a picture of pride, satisfaction, and achievement that is forever delicately painted in my memory. And though silent words of congratulations for a job well done were not verbally directed at me, I was able to witness the sense of joy, accomplishment, and success she was experiencing at that celebratory moment. That was her reward, her returns on the job she did at enforcing her value on education.

One unforgettable lesson that I continue to learn from my mother's hard-headed determination to secure us a high school education is that a plan B, or alternate plan of action, must be a major component of any serious undertaking, especially where cherished values are concerned. Her plan B was never mentioned, but she had it hidden away in that ever active mind of hers, ready to deploy, just in case.

It was no secret that my mother wanted us to attend one of the government secondary schools in Barbados. These historic and reputable institutions of learning, like Harrison College, Queen's College, Lodge, Combermere, Alexandra, Coleridge and Parry, The Alleyne School, and Foundation, were reputed to be the best, and parents beamed with pride and satisfaction when their sons and daughters were admitted to one of these fine institutions of academic notoriety.

These schools were prominent and well known for the prestigious place they occupied in the education system of Barbados. They were considered the cream of the crop, and their students were idolized as the best the island had to offer. And parents were justifiably proud and honored when their children were admitted. It shouldn't be at all surprising that my mother wanted so badly to be a member of that prestigious sect. But one or two hurdles had to be successfully cleared.

First, my Roebuck neighborhood did not send its youth to any of the schools I mentioned earlier. Not that it didn't want to. It just didn't. At least not in large numbers. It wasn't that we did not want to matriculate at these schools. We most definitely wanted to. I know I wanted to. And my mother wanted me to. But somehow, many of us did not make the cut. But that set of circumstances did not deter my mother in the least. She was determined that we would go to one of these schools. Her stubborn determination was one thing, but there were other factors at play.

By now, I was eleven, and the custom was that I, along with other boys and girls at that age across Barbados, had to take the eleven-plus exam. Some referred to it as the screening test. And that is exactly what it was - a test designed to screen out those who could not qualify for entrance to one of the prestigious government secondary grammar schools, based on their score on the assessment.

Those who didn't make the cut had to find another way to work towards a high school education. Many of us, including yours truly, did not make the passing score. While other parents and students from other neighborhoods across the island were rejoicing and celebrating, my mother, I, and others like us, were in the opposite mood. But before I delve into my mother's plan B that I referenced earlier, I digress to say a little about the state of mind that took hold of those of us that were screened out by the eleven-plus exam.

Personally, I was mortally wounded. At least, I felt that way. Wounded, because I had failed to qualify, but more so, because of the enormous disappointment my mother suffered, especially after the hopes and dreams she had invested on my behalf, and after the value she placed on education had taken such a direct and massive hit.

Needless to say, I internalized other thoughts and questions that were generated due to my poor performance. And I am sure that other boys and girls my age and in similar circumstances nursed similar thoughts and questions: Am I a dunce? Am I stupid? Am I not as smart as those who passed the test? What do others think of me? What do I do now? Is there any hope for me? What kind of future will I have?

But two competing and opposing strategies were happening simultaneously. While I was feeling sorry for myself, and the more I wrestled with finding credible answers to the questions I harbored inside, my mother, without uttering a single word, must have spoken quite loudly and eloquently concerning the tragedy that was inflicted on me and the many that shared my fate.

"It is a huge mistake," she must have said to herself, "to make a final decision on a child's educational future based on the results of one test and on one day's performance." In other words, the screening test was not going to define who I was, and the results of that single test fell way short of the actual measure of my personal worth and intelligence. And furthermore, those disappointing results could not in any way diminish the immense value she had placed on the worth of education.

My mother's value concerning the significance of education was too strong to allow the results I got on the eleven-plus exam to thwart or impede her plans for a high school education for me. Her convictions were too deeply rooted. Too guttural. Too deeply entrenched. She appeared to have questioned herself rhetorically: What's the worth of a value if the one who holds it bends, folds, and breaks at the first sign of interference or competition? And that's when her plan B took center stage.

I wish to make two crucial points before proceeding; two points that I hope would be forceful enough to lead you to more fully appreciate my mother's dogged and resolute stance on the value of education for her children. Whereas I previously wrote of the value my parents cherished concerning education, I now speak of education as being the value that was cherished by my mother. The reason for this change is the simple fact that by this time, my father had already migrated to the United Kingdom, and my mother was practically raising us on her own.

Secondly, it must be stated that my mother did not create a plan B because she knew I would fail the eleven-plus exam. She was too astute to engage in such a low level of thinking. Instead, she instituted the plan because it made good sense, and in doing so, she demonstrated a spirit of proactiveness that should be a component of serious planning on all fronts and in all spheres of business, leadership, and even parenting. She valued education too much to allow one setback to set her back. My education was going to happen in spite of this one hiccup, and the ease and comfort with which she announced her plan B told me that she had been thinking about it for some time.

"I am sending you to The Modern (High School)," she quietly announced one day. And that was it. She did not ask for my thoughts about the matter, and she did not invite a discussion. It was her plan. I had no say. All that was required of me was that I cooperate and go along with the plan as it unfolded; to go to school and learn, as my maternal grandmother so often counseled me; emphasizing *and learn,* as if to remind me that it was possible to go to school and not learn.

Even if I was given the opportunity to comment on the subject at hand, my first argument would have gone something like this: "But Muddah (mother), you have to pay to go there." But my mother's immediate and simple rebuttal would have been as quick as it was decisive. "I know that,"she would have replied. And that would have been the end of the conversation. This would have reinforced my thinking that she had already given adequate thought concerning the expense and the investment that such a plan would entail.

And what was even more striking about the entire plan, was the awareness that she was very exact concerning the specificity of the school she wanted me to attend. Just any school would not do. The value she placed on education would not allow her to settle for less than the best.

Of the almost countless number of private schools in operation on the island, she had chosen The Modern. And her sureness and resolute conviction told me that she had done her homework in researching the academic record of these schools, and was sure that she had made the correct decision for her. And for me. She had done her own screening and had screened out those that did not make the cut.

I am absolutely certain that her unmistakable value on education was the guiding principle that led her to a final decision. That principle must have driven her into inquiry mode and forced her to internalize many questions before settling on her irreversible decision: What is the success record of each school's graduates? What are the qualifications of the staff? What values does the leadership of each school possess? Is the curriculum current? Are the expectations rigorous enough, and compare favorably to that of the government schools that were mentioned previously?

It is one thing to speak eloquently about a value one may possess. But it is another thing to do what it takes to protect and perpetuate that cherished value. Without a doubt, my mother bravely demonstrated both virtues, especially in light of the reality that education at her chosen school was not free, as it was at the government schools. Even though this new budget item would have been strenuous on an already stretched-to-the-limit financial situation, her value on education remained a priority and a necessity.

As the saying goes, she put her money where her mouth was, even though she was not blessed to have an endless supply of money. But having said that, I am sure that she must have already prayed, planned, and strategized on best practices to fund the newly added line item to an already tight budget. She must have concluded that education for me and my siblings was too important an investment to allow money, or the lack of it, to stand as a barrier. Reflecting on those days, I vividly recall how she went without her own personal needs and how she threw an extra meeting hand to ensure that she had my school fees on hand when it was due.

For obvious reasons, I don't think it is worth the time to go into extensive detail concerning my history at my new school, but I wish to elaborate a little on those initial moves that my mother put in place to get the visible and the public portion of her value started. One Saturday morning in 1962, she engaged the services of her sister, my Aunt Gloria, to accompany me to The Modern High School to take the entrance exam, which I recall was not too challenging. When all was said and done, I was confident that I had passed and that I would be accepted.

I was jubilant when I enrolled the following September to embark on my high school academic career, as well as on a journey that would create unforgettable memories that will be certain to last a lifetime. I jumped almost immediately into the school's thriving track and field program, in which I achieved modest success, but it was an experience that brought with it a bunch of friends, lasting memories, and countless celebrations; one of the many spin off values that my mother didn't perceive as part of her initial value.

My academic performance was not stellar, but I considered it to be at least commendable, especially when compared to many of the exceptionally talented and academically gifted students I encountered. But it was good enough for my mother as long as I brought home good marks on my report card. She was excited about the attention I attracted, due to my participation in track and field and cross country, and the recognition she received as a result of my success and popularity. But she remained steadfastly focused on the value of academic preparation. While she was proud of me for winning medals and trophies, she consistently protected the value she had on education by ensuring that I had all the tools, books, and uniforms necessary for success.

But nowhere in the process was she more focused, serious and intentional than the nightly homework and study routine. Her work on perpetuating her value on education was not done when I entered high school. She took it to another level, and closely and personally supervised the session to the point where she made sure that homework time each night was dedicated, quiet and respected.

As I write this, I can't help but remember how she made sure that when it came to homework, the house had to be quiet, the radio turned off, and all unnecessary movement and chatting by siblings held to a minimum. "Sylvester is studying," she would announce, as she demanded the same study environment that was in place for my older sister, Elaine.

Understandably, she did not stay up late for the lengthy study periods but she made sure that my homework was getting my attention before she went off to a well-deserved sleep. Although her sleep routine happened nightly, there is one time I can recall her pulling an all-nighter with me on one special occasion.

It was a Saturday night and my school leaving (GCE) exam in Biology (my favorite subject) was scheduled for the following Monday. Plus I had a track and field event on the same day. I can't remember if I had requested her company or if she volunteered to stay up with me, keeping my company while I studied.

As expected, she didn't last too long but she remained at her post with me, only falling off to sleep after she did not have the energy to continue, leaving the music of her snoring to represent her presence. Her spirit was willing but her flesh was weak, but it was the absolute personification of the value she represented. In case you are wondering about the results of the athletic event and the Biology exam, I won the 800 meters before making my way across the city to The Springer Memorial School, where I took and passed my Biology exam. What a day!

She did what she could, with an understanding that she was not equipped to lend not even the smallest iota of academic assistance in English, Math, Literature, French, or Biology, in which I excelled. Still, she persisted passionately and dauntlessly, with one hundred percent support and encouragement.

In the end, my high school years at The Modern ended with a measure of academic success, which was good enough to earn me a position as an elementary school teacher at All Saints Boys School. Needless to say, my mother was elated, even though her jubilation was measured and quiet. This was what she had worked for. She had seen her work and her value of education on my behalf vindicated. Her jubilation and satisfaction were on full display when I emerged from my room dressed in a shirt and tie to report for duty at All Saints on that very first morning of my teaching career. It was 'mission accomplished' for her.

However, alongside my academic and athletic achievements at The Modern High School, a stark realization and a glaring revelation were happening that was impossible to miss. It was the flagrant and blatant reality that at my school were scores of students who were just like me in at least two ways. Without a doubt, each student there was from a home where education was valued. Like me, they had a mother or a father, or both, that like my mother, had placed a high value on education, and who were just as ardent and zealous as far as placing a high school education within reach of their children.

Secondly, and most importantly, my fellow students at my new school and I knew only too well of the stigma that was attached to us because of us failing the dreaded screening test. For the vast majority of us, that was why we ended up at The Modern as 'second-class citizens' in the first place. Nevertheless, it was remarkable to observe the level of vindication, as well as the exoneration that was literally emerging before my very eyes, day after day, and year after year, for as long as I remained at that school.

Fortunately, I kept company with a bunch of motivated, talented, and bright students, who felt that they had something to prove; that they were academically just as good or better than their counterparts in the government schools across town and across the island, who had passed the screening test.

As a result, they immersed themselves in their studies with such fervor and energy that it resulted in unparalleled success when the results of nationwide school-leaving exam results were returned. My results were moderate compared to many of my schoolmates, who outperformed many in the government schools and the other private high schools in Barbados.

In all fairness, and to our advantage, we had a reputable principal whose diction would often send us scurrying to consult a dictionary. And we were blessed to have a teaching staff that was qualified and determined. Is it any wonder that my mother's value of education directed her to this school?

On an exceptional level, I rubbed shoulders with students that exhibited a natural brilliance and an uncanny capacity to grapple with, understand, and master the most complicated content in math, the sciences, foreign languages, athletics, and a variety of areas. And yet, we had one thing in common. We had all failed the common entrance exam, or the screening test, or the eleven plus assessment, however you wish to name the thing.

What a paradoxical state of affairs! But this irony was not lost or wasted. It taught a valuable lesson and a moral which my mother and those like her embraced; that one setback on one day was not powerful enough to derail their value on education or sufficiently compelling to nullify the educational goals they had for their children.

My mother and the other parents entrusted their failing youngsters to the care of The Modern High School, at a time when we felt damaged and hopeless. But because the immense value they placed on education was so sturdy and compelling, a single defeat was not enough to alter their educational goals for us. Rather, it turned out to be the perfect mechanism they used to shore up their resolve to do whatever it took to make their value real in our lives.

That lesson and moral remain just as potent today as it was for me back in 1962, and is one that is applicable to every young person everywhere; that one initial failure in anything, be it education, sports, or love, is not to be interpreted as an end to one's hopes, dreams, and aspirations, but should be seen as an invitation to pursue alternatives to build on the values that they have always had.

That was the very attitude and value that drove my mother to enroll me in The Modern High School. And other mothers and fathers were certainly guided by a similar value that they too placed on education. I am proud to add that so many of my schoolmates, who like me, failed the screening test, and who were dubbed as not good enough or smart enough, went on to hold positions of leadership, influence, and responsibility in Barbados, regionally, and on the international stage as well, in spite of the one initial failure.

Accordingly, if it were possible to interview my mother concerning the value she placed on education, she would have stated very briefly that she valued education so that her children would *turn out* better than she did. I made certain to mention the phrase, turn out, simply because it was exactly what I heard coming from her very mouth from time to time. It was her way of reminding us of the value she treasured and the investment she was making on our behalf. It was also her way of reminding us of the part we had to play in making sure that we did turn out better than she did.

Carefully and overtly implied in her *turn out* comment was the crux of her fixation on education and what she wanted it to do for us. What she really meant by turn out was that education was a road out of poverty.

And if she was pushed to further expand on the reason for her value of and support for education, Iola Mayers would have said that she wanted a high school education for her children because it would allow them to be independent, responsible, and to provide for themselves.

At the end of the day, my mother's investment in my education and that of my four sister siblings, paid huge dividends. To say she was proud as she reaped the fruits of her labor is an understatement. Her relentless value translated into the making of two nurses, one physical therapist, one business professional, and one educator. Most of us are now retired, and we all remain grateful and thankful for a mother and her value that was well spent.

<u>Extended Value-added Thinking and Action:</u>

1. I just told the story of the value my mother placed on education. Write your personal story from the perspective of a parent or from that of a student. How does your story differ from mine? In what ways is it similar?

2. Make a list of at least five prominent figures, and do a search to discover their obstacles and failures before they became successful. Include a statement detailing what you have learned from each person's experience and how it impacted you.

3. Make a conscious effort to seek out someone that is experiencing failure and setbacks while pursuing a worthy goal relative to a value you hold dear. What kind of involvement do you plan to pursue to assist this person in reaching his or her desired outcome?

Chapter 5
Show Some Respect

Respect for ourselves guides our morals. Respect for others guides our manners.

-Laurence Stern

After reading the three previous chapters in which there was a full-blown expose of the values my mother held dear, readers may be wondering how many more she could contain. Truth be told, the values that have received thorough attention previously, along with the ones to be featured in this chapter, were, for the most part, the values of most parents that resided in my small community in Roebuck, Barbados. My mother, and my father, to some extent, only get special mention because they were the ones responsible for making their values play out on behalf of my siblings and me. And so, it is rather safe to say that my friends that grew up with me would write stories that approximate mine.

We grew up knowing that respect for others was a priority in our modest home. But the level of respect we were expected to give far exceeded the walls of our small house. The smallness and simplicity of the house were in no way a predictor of the nature and quality of the respect we were expected to display from day to day. In fact, it was this unspoken lesson that we learned from early

- the poorer we were, the more respectful we should strive to be. Paying respect was an important value that was held in high esteem by my parents and the other parents in the community.

Respect began at home. In many respects, most lessons in just about everything, were caught and taught at home. But having said that, it must be made clear that there were no sit-down formal teachings by my parents on how to be respectful. And even though it was a learning environment in our home classroom, our parents did not pull out a published text or manual with carefully written content and research on the value of respect, and how to teach it to small children. Still, it was taught and practiced with regularity.

Honestly, I can't recall how old I was when I began saying thank you, or, yes, please, or covering my sneeze or cough, or even saying please for a pass (may I have a pass, please?). My only conclusion is that I caught those aspects of respect from my older sister, Elaine. My parents must have taught her via direct instruction, and like the good student she was, she must have passed those values down to me, which I passed to Yvonne and Yvonne to Cheryl, who passed them on to Heather (Neats). Bear in mind that I am only thinking out loud concerning this osmosis-like process, without having a definitive answer, but conventional wisdom must prevail at this point.

Even though my parents valued respect and regarded it very highly, they hardly used the word. It is hard to believe, but it is true. In fact, I am going out on a limb and confirm that I have never heard them ever use the word. They may have, but I am one hundred percent accurate in my thinking. And one would think that they would have repeated the word over and over since it was a value they respected, and one on which they worked very hard to make it our personal value as well.

However, there was one word I heard them utter on a regular basis - manners. To them, there were good manners, and then there were bad ones. Obviously, they wanted us to have good manners because it meant that we had respect. So, when we said excuse me, we were demonstrating good manners. And when we covered our cough or sneeze with our hands, that was good manners.

But we had bad manners or were unmannerly when we made that mushy sound while talking with food in our mouth, or did not say yes please or no please when answering them, our grandmother, our teachers, or anyone that was older or in authority. And it was never just yes or no for us. It always had to be yes please, and no please. That was the accepted and expected culture of respect in Roebuck. To behave otherwise would have been unmannerly and disrespectful.

It must be clear by now that my parents viewed manners and respect as synonymous terms. When they confronted us with "you have no manners," they certainly meant that we were not respectful. And they valued respect too much to let us get away with disrespectful behavior. Just as they valued work, education, and church attendance, and worked hard to have them replicated in us, so too they valued respect for others and were just as adamant in their expectations as far as our having respect for others was concerned.

After all, what good would it be if we valued education, attended church regularly, valued hard work, and lacked respect and good manners? That thought pattern must have been my parents' attitude as far as the connectivity of their values was concerned.

Respect for one another was a house rule, but respect for others was one character trait that, to them, was the eleventh commandment, it went something like this – "Thou shalt not disrespect other persons that do not live in this house, especially if they are older. Thou shalt say good morning or good evening to them when you pass them on the street, see them in the shop or encounter them at the pipe."

So, there was no misunderstanding between my siblings and me concerning the behavior standards and level of respect they valued, exacted, and expected from us towards others. It was a serious breach of protocol, when even the slightest incident of disrespect or bad manners was shown toward others, especially the older people in the neighborhood. Any reported infringement was usually met with immediate, harsh, and sometimes painful consequences.

Simply put, there were some infractions against the respectful and mannerly protocols that we could get away with every once in a while. But there were others that drew the ire of the respect police that were always on duty in our home. Yelling at one another may have received a simple warning every now and then. And forgetting to say yes please, and no please might have been reinforced by a stern look. So were violations such as talking mean to one another or the ever-present sibling rivalry. However, other disrespectful and unmannerly conduct of an inexcusable nature was never tolerated and was greeted with the appropriate justice mixed with a lot less mercy.

Talking back to my mother was like a death sentence. Incidentally, I recently ran across the following statement while scrolling through social media on my cell phone. It went something like this. "When I was growing up, there were two ways to die. One was by natural causes, and disrespecting my parents was the other." I chuckled to myself, realizing how accurately it supports the statement I posited a moment ago. We knew that, and were smart enough to seek refuge out of the reach of any missile or projectile that was in their reach.

Talking back was the ultimate disrespectful act we could do, and if we were in close proximity to our parents while engaging in mouthing off to them, they got their hands on us, and the outcome was never good. And even if I ran away to escape the consequences, I still had to come home to sleep when night came. I learned early to take the punishment immediately. Getting it over and done with was my strategy. Thinking of the night encounters was too taxing on my mental state if I spent all day wondering what the night meeting would be like.

While writing this, I am enjoying a personal and private laugh as I muse on an encounter I had with my mother. I was about sixteen at the time of this almost fateful incident. I was taking a bath outside one morning when my mother asked me to do a chore after my bath and before I left the house. My recollections concerning her request and my response are sketchy, but I obviously talked back or made a disrespectful comment. I was quick enough to get out of the way of an identified flying object.

My mother didn't play when disrespectful and unmannerly behavior was our response to her directives. She took parenting very seriously, and even more seriously after my father migrated to the United Kingdom and she was raising us on her own. It was as if she welcomed the opportunity to demonstrate her strong leadership skills of reinforcing the family's values on her own.

My mother, like all or most mothers in Roebuck, was very quick to pick up on both verbal and nonverbal forms of disrespect, and she moved immediately and decisively to stamp them out. Muttering under our breath as a response to her directive was never a safe thing to do. "What did you say? She would ask. "Nothing," was the usual reply. But she knew better than that. Even a certain look she did not appreciate was interpreted as disrespectful, unmannerly, and rude.

My sister, Elaine, remembers looking cross-eyed at our mother one day, and as she said, "I pushed up my mouth at her. It did not end well." It only goes to show how deadly defiance and disrespect that was leveled at her could be. Respect for others was one of her major values, and she stopped at nothing to enforce it, even if she had to employ extreme methods.

My second sister, Yvonne, also tells her story of an encounter she had with my mother and how she suffered the consequences of talking back. If you recall, I went into a rather lengthy discussion in a previous chapter on the value of church attendance that my parents held very seriously. One aspect of that value that I did not mention was that our behavior in church mattered, and that the value was seriously devalued if our behavior at church was not up to par.

Apparently, as told by Yvonne, she and a friend of hers had been talking way too much in church, too much talking as per our mother's standards for church decorum. When confronted by my mother at home after church about her talking, Yvonne proceeded to talk back, telling my mother that she was old enough and that she could make her own decisions. Furthermore, she added the comment that she was a working woman, suggesting that she was grown and that she was outside the boundaries of parental control. I don't know what possessed her to talk back. But I do know what happened to her. According to Yvonne, she, too, suffered the consequences that were in place for talking back.

I was not privy to the encounter Yvonne had with our mother, but I think I am absolutely correct in describing my mother's reaction. "You talking back to me? Not in my house… As long as you are living under my roof, you will do as I say. I don't care how old you are or if you are working. This is my house and…." That back and forth between Yvonne and our mother proved two things; that my mother had the final word and that it didn't matter how old we were, respect for our parents was an expectation, and we dared not mount a challenge as long as we were living under their roof.

As far as my parents were concerned, lying to them was a serious breach of their respect protocols. Many people may not see it in the same light or as a respect issue, but my parents seriously held fast to their stance and abhorred the practice of lying, punishing it soundly when it happened.

They appeared to have received their inspiration on the seriousness of lying from the Bible itself. Proverbs 12:22 to be exact: *Lying lips are an abomination to the Lord: but they that deal truly are his delight.* If it was an abomination to God, then it was one to them as well. I was to find out the hard way how serious the consequences were for committing this specific abomination. I told this very story in my previous book, *It's Your Word Against Mine*, but I am repeating it here in a different context.

One Sunday morning, I took the sheep out to graze, as was my custom. On the day in question, I took the small flock to an unusual grazing spot that had a lot of brush, where an unfortunate turn of events happened. One of the sheep got tangled in the brush and hung itself. When I returned to the grazing spot around midday to move the sheep to another grazing spot and discovered the tragedy, I went into full deception mode, dragging the dead sheep to the spot where it should have been in the first place, returning home feeling quite good about myself, that I had covered up my sin.

Unfortunately for me, my lie confronted me soon after that. Mr. Worrell had come across the dead sheep before it was moved and had already shared the news with my father. Without alerting me that he had been in conversation with Mr. Worrell, he asked me the obvious question as soon as he got home. "Where did you take the sheep today? he asked me. "Down to Midfield," I replied. "And what happened to the sheep that died?" he continued. "When I went back to look for the sheep, I found that one had died, and I don't know why," I concluded. He then went on to tell me that I was lying, that I had not taken the sheep to Midfield as I had said, and that Mr. Worrell had come across the hung sheep tangled up in the bushes. I had no defense to his cross-examination and paid the price by receiving severe flogging.

The story I shared above was done so that readers arrive at the conclusion that my father, as well as my mother, did not tolerate being lied to, whether in small or large matters. They had already been in solid agreement that lying to them was a matter of disrespect, which was directly opposed to their value of respect for themselves and others. Furthermore, I had not only lied but was also dishonest and deceptive, behaviors that were just as serious.

If you are thinking that lying and talking back to my parents were the only disrespectful behaviors that my siblings and I tried to get away with, you have to think again. There were others that were just as dangerous and insidious. But my parents and the others in Roebuck appeared united in their efforts to eradicate them at all costs.

One such act of utter disrespect was disobedience. And they were just as quick and decisive to deal with this wrong. Willful disobedience and defiance were like a disease that could spread if left unchecked and unmonitored. And they had the precise medicine and therapeutics to prevent its spread outside the home to the school, church, and to the wider community.

They valued respect too highly to allow disobedience and obstinance to take root and metastasize. Bear in mind that we weren't that bold and brazen to respond with an outright no to a directive from our parents.

That would have been suicidal and foolish. But simply refusing to do what they instructed was just as reckless. Here is a case in point.

One Ash Wednesday, a group of us went about our job of taking out the sheep to graze in Midfield on Sedgepond Plantation, just down the hill from where we lived in Roebuck. This day was different in that it was a holiday. We did not have to rush back to go to school. It was also different in another respect. Our parents were home from work and were preparing for the usual Ash Wednesday all-day prayer service at the local New Testament Church.

Before we set out, the command from our parents was not to "spend the whole day down there." We found a suitable grazing spot for the sheep, and before we knew it, we were at the river catching crayfish and throwing them into a container of water for safekeeping until we got back home.

Apparently, we were having too much fun to notice that the time was far spent. Sedgepond was a home away from home for us, especially when school was out. We could fish, climb coconut trees, suck sugar cane, feast on fat pork and cashews, and enjoy eating from the occasional bunch of ripe bananas. The comfort level was comfortable and entertaining for a group of adventurous and rambunctious early teenagers that were at home in the wild.

No wonder we were caught off guard when the sun began to set. We had not planned to disobey, but we had. We knew we were in trouble and sought ways to appease the impending wrath. At the time, we cooked on an outdoor fireplace, and each of us felt that if we each collected a bundle of firewood, it would soften the blow. So, we grabbed our sheep and wood, and with the catch of crayfish secure in the bucket, we cautiously began our climb of Sedgepond Hill towards home.

Ms. Morris, Carson's mother, was the first to meet us. And she did not even utter one word of condemnation. Initially, I thought she was kissing him. That was until I heard him scream. She was biting his ear. He was 'hard ears,' a term our parents used when we were disobedient. She also took the time to fling our catch of the day into the brush nearby.

Michael's dad met us next, and he got it right there. So did Livingstone (Robin Hood). My father was the last to meet us. And I hated that because while my partners in crime were cooling off from their ordeal, while mine was yet to come. I didn't have long to wait for my encounter. It didn't matter that hehad just spent an entire day praying and fasting at church, no doubt praying for us to be obedient and respectful. I had undermined a family value and had to suffer the consequences.

Respect and obedience were values they seriously embraced, and they were dedicated to enforcing them at all cost, even if they contracted the help of the church's assistance.

Another sister, Cheryl, also had to learn the hard way that disobeying my mother was both foolhardy and unsafe, even in the little things that may have appeared insignificant and trifling. According to Cheryl's accounting of the infraction, she was told by my mother to take the school bus home from school. A very simple but direct request. And as far as my mother was concerned, it was not a suggestion or even an option. As per Cheryl's tale, she and a friend decided to take a regular passenger bus instead. Not a wise decision. After all, a bus is a bus. What's the difference? Cheryl continues, "when I stepped in the house, she was there waiting for me." And the rest is history.

At that point in time, the bus was not the focal point. As far as my mother was concerned, Cheryl's disobedience was a severe breach of the respect protocol, and her act of defiance against my mother and her request, no matter how simple, was not going to be tolerated.

The incidents mentioned above are an indication of how seriously respect was valued, especially where disobedience was concerned. As is the case with lying, my parents and her cohorts also relied heavily on the Bible for their authority to stamp out the disrespectful act of disobedience: *Children obey your parents in the Lord,* it says in Ephesians 6:1-3, *for this is right. Honor thy father and mother… That it may be well with thee, and thou mayest live on the earth.* The authority and command included in that verse were their marching orders, and they perceived it as the gospel that it was.

Fortunately, there were some respectful behaviors that my parents had no problems at all reinforcing. That made their work much easier. And to their credit, they practiced what they preached. The mantra that they appeared to have adopted was *do as I do and do as I say.* The point I am trying to make is a very simple one. They did not curse and swear or use vulgar language at all, whether in our presence or in general. It was not like them. It was not who they were. I don't even think that they knew how to curse and swear. Particularly my mother. She would have looked and sounded utterly awkward, cursing and swearing. They respected us that much, and we returned the favor. To be absolutely transparent, I picked up a few curse words along the way but never really used them in conversation with my friends, far less in earshot of my parents.

And secondly, we were respectful to our parents in other ways as well. I would have not only disappointed them but disrespected them as well if I smoked or drank. Here again, they were the examples. I never saw my father smoke a cigarette or drink rum, behaviors that were very common among men in my neighborhood and the surrounding ones.

I never expected my mother to engage in smoking and drinking. Had she done that, she would have been in the minority among her fellow women, and would have been castigated and shamed.

So, as a teenager, after my father, the male influence in my life, migrated to the United Kingdom, if I had one night walked into our home with alcohol and nicotine on my breath, that would have been very disrespectful to my mother. And she wouldn't have stood for that. And that first time would have been my last because of the unforgettable scourging that would be mine.

The truth is that boys my age did not engage in that kind of behavior. There appeared to have been an unspoken stipulation that smoking and drinking were adult behaviors and that young boys my age were not invited. Even if, at some point, I had harbored thoughts of stealing a sip every now and again, the sight of grown inebriated men stumbling and uttering undecipherable gibberish on the way home from the rum shop would have been a strong deterrent.

It goes without saying that my parents had a much broader goal. While their primary purpose was to raise respectful children who knew how to be civil and cultural at home, their ultimate target was molding their offspring to behave mannerly, polished, and respectfully in public.

Our home was the training ground, the first classroom, and they were our first teachers. To them, training in the art of respectfulness and obedience was just as important as mastering reading, writing, and arithmetic skills. They were very mindful that our public deportment, whether good or otherwise, was a direct and personal reflection on them and the nature of the training, discipline, and guidance they dispensed at home. We, too, were just as aware that once we stepped foot out the door, we represented them, and were Fred and Iola's children.

And so, a special brand of behavior was expected of us once we were outside the boundaries of our home and in the broader sphere of the neighborhood, the school, the streets, the shop, and at the local standpipe where we collected water in buckets to carry on our heads back to the house.

The level of respect that was to be extended to older persons in the neighborhood was not to be misunderstood or forgotten. The protocol called for us to say good morning or good evening to every older person we met. "Good morning Mr. Marshall. Good evening Ms. Watson. Good night Brother Scant." That was the respect due them. And they expected it. And my parents modeled it and expected it from us. That was their value, and if we did not deliver, it got back to them swiftly. "Sylvester didn't speak to me this morning," one would complain. Or "he walked past me and stared in my face and did not speak," another might have protested. And once messages like those got back to my parents, it was never a good situation to be in.

And no first names either. It had to be Mr. This and Ms. That. I would have been out of my mind to refer to Gerald Lowe as Gerald. Or to Mrs. Headley as Irmina. Or to Ms. St. Hill as Norma. That would have been a serious mistake and would be classified as a disrespectful act of the highest order. It would get back to my parents, and it would turn out to be an uncomfortable situation for us to be in.

Married people got that special respect, but others still had to be respected by being greeted and hailed in a respectful manner. As long as they were older, our parents' value of respect was due to them, male or female. One thing was clear. Our parents' respect protocol, as far as older people were concerned, was that we were to be the ones to initiate the greetings.

Total respect meant that the youth were the ones to speak first and that the older residents, by virtue of their age, experience, and wisdom, had earned the prestige and honor to be so recognized and respected. And we bestowed it on them whether we wanted to or not. We just had to. It was not just an overt mark of respect. It was the culture of the neighborhood. A culture that was passed down from generations. My parents did not want to be guilty of causing a breach of a long-standing cultural custom, so they did their part to maintain the status quo.

Having said what I just wrote, I have often wondered what effect it had on the psyche of the older residents in the neighborhood when they were greeted with a hearty good morning or an exuberant good evening and other forms of respectful behavior coming from us. I have thought about that for a while, and even more so since I began writing the book, and have been able to come to a conclusion based on my experience, since I became an older person. So here it is. Maybe you will agree, or you may not.

When a young person meets me in my neighborhood and, without prompting, recognizes me with a cheery hello, hi, or even a spirited wave of the hand, it does something to me. It affirms that I am a human being that has a basic need to be recognized. It also confirms that I have value and worth, and that a mere hello from a stranger, a neighbor, or even some random person who takes the time to recognize me, supports the need to feel needed and important.

I feel better about myself whenever that happens. I can't explain the psychology of the experience, but I know all too well of the power of a hello or a good morning. And to be fortunate enough to receive a free, generous, and simple greeting, especially when I am not expecting it, is life-changing and a truly beautiful thing.

Isn't there any wonder why my parents so vigorously perpetuated the value of respect for others? They had to know from their own experience how the impact of good morning, good evening, and hello had on the older men and women in our community. And it had not so much to do with age or seniority as it had to do with the feeling of well-being it brought to the lives of those fortunate enough to welcome it.

But knowing my parents as I do and the Christian and religious fervor that informed their approach to life, they must have discovered an additional reason for voluntarily respecting our more mature residents by offering a simple greeting, whether early in the morning, at midday, or late in the evening. They saw others as creatures created in God's image and deserving of the treatment and respect reserved for all His children. That's why they chose respect as a value and the supreme motivation for influencing us to do the same.

Similarly, respecting others heaped benefits on the one doing the giving. And as I mentioned previously, my personal experience bears this out. I felt really good and accomplished each time I greeted an older person using the required respectful format and protocol that my parents put in place. First, I was accomplishing the use of their value, simultaneously bearing in mind that the complimentary comment that I had good manners would often get back to my parents. "Sylvester spoke to me this morning," one might report back. Secondly, to hear the older folk respond in kind to my greetings was very affirming and, in turn, showed their respect for me. But most important of all was the assurance that because I demonstrated respect and good manners, I was responsible for positively impacting the life and well-being of another person.

It is also interesting and quite remarkable how my parents promoted the respect value, and the other spin-off benefits and unexpected rewards. As mentioned previously, I was able to observe how respect begets respect and how the seniors and the younger residents in the neighborhood mutually benefited from the respect culture that our parents and the others engineered in Roebuck.

Everyone knew everyone by name and the sound of good morning was as popular and as refreshing as the smell of bakes deep frying in lard oil early in the morning. The wet of fallen dew, and the organized chaos caused by countless sheep and cows, along with their would-be teenage farmers and seasoned workers cluttering the narrow street at sunrise on the way to the grazing grounds on Sedgepond Plantation created the perfect scenario and venue that encouraged and supported the value of respect.

Good morning and good evening filled the air as young and old alike reveled in the atmosphere of respect and recognition, some dispensing, others receiving. It was almost magical as the people of our small agricultural district used the value of respect for all as a starting point to bring the community together. The closest I have come to anything like it is the similar atmosphere that was created daily in a professional situation where the jolly sounds of good morning could be heard in the school houses where I worked, as teachers greeted each other as they arrived for the start of the day's work.

It is rather interesting to discover that research supports my premise, and to some extent, that of my parents, that greeting others with a hearty and respectful good morning has its benefits. My parents thought that saying good morning was simply a display of good manners. Interestingly enough, research by Lindsay Dodgson specifically mentions good manners as one of the eight reasons you should always say good morning to your coworkers. Included in the eight reasons are the following: it is basic manners; it humanizes; it creates a democratic environment; it is quick; it is free; you might get noticed yourself; it reduces awkwardness; and it might cheer someone up.

Even the less formal hello has its benefits. To be clear, my parents' value of respect, especially for the older residents of Roebuck, was the formal approach. The good morning approach. To them, the hello approach was too informal. Too casual. Saying hi or hello to Mr. Cox or Mrs. Straker was much too familiar and was reserved for friends, and for those who had not yet reached seniority status.

But, as mentioned before, the latter also had its advantages. I took the time to see what google has to say about the benefits of saying hello. Here is what I discovered. "Saying hello gives you confidence and optimism. Most of the time, when you say hello, that greeting is returned. This little success promotes confidence within and teaches you that people don't bite. It is a sign of respect. It is a sign of being friendly. It is a way of telling the other person they exist, and acknowledging them…."

Be that as it may, the picture painted above, as pretty as it was, had some special shades and hues of respect that were distributed in select places and extra special people across the local landscape and beyond. Simply put, although I showed great respect and good manners to the older residents in our neighborhood, there were some that, for one reason or another, received special attention as far as my respect was concerned.

And this was not a departure from my parents' value that respect be shown to all. They did not teach us to pick and choose who to respect. The expectation was that we respect everyone, irrespective of where they worked, if they went to church, or if they were male or female. But as far as I was concerned, the unequal way in which I distributed my respect in this instance was unavoidable.

The fact is that several persons in our neighborhood impacted me more than others; those that developed more than a good morning or good evening relationship with me. The value my mother placed on respect was so transparent that I found it rather easy to pay respect to others in our community, and to seek out those that were leaders and examples living among us. I pause here to single out a few of them. I refer to them as lighthouses.

One such lighthouse that I respected beyond measure was Alphonso Scantlebury. And to be honest, I know for sure that he respected me as well. Affectionately known as Brother Scant, because of his membership in The Roebuck New Testament Church, Brother Scant lived up to his name and title. To me, he was an example of what a true Christian should be. And anyone, man or woman, boy or girl, who was seriously looking for a mentor in good clean Christian living found it in Brother Scant. I respected him for his attitude toward parenting. I have never heard him raise his voice to anyone, including his children. He spoke sternly but did it softly, with grace and respect.

I was so sure about his gentle spirit and welcoming demeanor that I would show up at his home anytime and without invitation. Some homes were not open to just anyone, but Brother Scant's was not one of them. He was so down-to-earth and accessible. As a matter of full disclosure, Brother Scant was married to Aunt Rita, my father's sister. But I am confident the welcome would have been extended even if we were not connected as relatives. Brother Scant was as humorous as he was tall and lanky. He was a devout family man full of love for his wife and children and with much love left over for anyone else who needed the nurturing and support of an older Christian gentleman.

I was always impressed with how he publicly demonstrated his brand of Christianity, and I respected that more than any other trait he was so blessed to possess. He was not one to be melancholy and sad looking but chose to use his smile, his laughter, and his friendly personality as tools for witnessing to others about the God he served and loved. I have come across persons who identified themselves as Christians and felt that a sour and uninviting countenance was a hallmark of Christian living. This is not to say that Bro. Scant was not serious-minded or deeply religious. He was that and more. He was approachable, so much so that I was never afraid or timid around him.

Additionally, I respected Brother Scant on yet another level: church attendance. As you have read before, church attendance was a value my parents practiced, and they saw to it that we did the same. So, it is not difficult to understand the ease with which we connected and respected one another. He was always at church when services were scheduled. That was laudable.

But church attendance was just the beginning as far as Brother Scant was concerned. He taught Sunday School regularly, and he preached often. I am not sure if he was ever officially elected the assistant to Pastor Sobers, but that was the impression I always had of him.

He was a leader who was respected, not only by me, but by the congregation and the entire community. Brother Scant's church behavior was exemplary. I always admired and respected him for his punctuality and the way he conducted himself in the Lord's house. Always reverent but never pretentious or with a holier-than-thou attitude. It may be a stretch worth considering, but my present involvement in my church might have had its beginnings from observing Brother Scant's church activities so many years ago.

One more thing. My respect for Brother Scant rose precipitously when I considered how much he was able to do and the many he was able to influence, bearing in mind the limited academic and professional experience and preparation he had. Still, he knew his Bible and was very comfortable expounding from the pulpit. He sought to learn more and never let his lack of a first-class education deter him from serving, leading, or getting better and more enlightened.

The lessons he taught, whether unconscious or intentional, were striking and memorable. The premise that one does not have to be 'educated' to make a difference, or to serve, or to make a healthy impact is certainly true in Brother Scant's case, and his accomplishments and service to our local community deserve all the respect and attention they have received from me and from everyone else.

Outside of church, Bro. Scant was a regular person: congenial, law-abiding, and good-natured, with an attitude that said he was not better than anyone else. And I observed and respected him for that. Above all, he worked hard to support his family, another value my parents espoused and strongly encouraged my siblings and me to adopt.

Like my mother and many others from Roebuck, Brother Scant toiled on the plantation without complaint, harvesting sugar cane and planting and caring for the plantation's produce of yams, potatoes, bananas, cassava, and the rest. Simultaneously, he cared for his plot of land, where he grew his own food to feed his family and formed a business relationship with his wife, my Aunt Rita, in which she hawked the produce from the land in Speightstown every week.

He loved family gatherings. And this aspect of his personality must have been an encouragement to all because it was on full display for all to see. From him, I learned the importance of family and the father's role in bringing the family together to celebrate or be together for the sake of being together. My sisters and I would drop by from time to time to socialize with our cousins. His open arms of welcome were always outstretched, and we reciprocated with laughter and a healthy appetite because food was always a part of the proceedings.

At no other time was his family spirit more prominent than at Christmas. And my respect for him grew even more at this festive time of the year. He reveled in the festive atmosphere, and it appeared as if his best Christmas gift was the sight of his family enjoying the blessings of the yuletide season. He was special. He was what Steve Pemberton called a Lighthouse because of the influence and positive impact he had on me and others.

Farley Marshall was another lighthouse, and an older gentleman I grew to respect. I refer to him as Farley in this setting, but I dared not call him Farley back then. The respect level was too elevated to even think about it. He was always Mr. Marshall for me and to those like me. And his wife, Iris, was similarly thought of and as highly respected. Although not the spiritual influence for which Brother Scant was known, he too was a church man, choosing to cross the border into nearby Indian Ground to attend the Christian Mission Church there.

Nevertheless, he commanded respect without fanfare or flourish. Always a gentleman, without scandal or immoral conduct, he too was a model of dedication to his wife and children. Although I was never privy to any of his fatherly conversations with them, I got the idea that he, too, valued education because, like my mother, he sacrificed to make a secondary education possible for his children. He was the kind of father who encouraged his children by constantly reminding them that they could become anything they wanted.

As I write, I can't help but conclude that the other youngsters, like me, held Mr. Marshall in similar esteem because of who he was, and how he always displayed a fatherly attitude towards all of us. Especially me, since I was friendly with one of his daughters. Even in that situation, my respect for him was not built on fear but on the truth that he was such an honorable gentleman that boys my age admired.

I recall how he used to sit at his window and watch the neighborhood boys play street cricket in front of his house, even though the house suffered a hit from a stray ball every now and then, and even a broken window pane once or twice. The grace with which he handled those incidents was admirable, even though there was damage to his property. I am sure he could have found many other things to do, but he let us entertain him after a day's work. And to have had the honor of having him as a spectator at our youthful games was a distinction that all of us remember to this day, I am sure.

Unlike Brother Scant, Mr. Marshall did not work on the plantation, planting and harvesting sugar cane (cutting canes, as we said back then). But that doesn't mean he did not value hard work that was common among the people in Roebuck at the time. Far from it. He and his family owned a plot of land close to the house. I am reflecting as I write, and I have concluded that the small space was probably the most productive per square foot in Roebuck. It produced a variety of fruits for family consumption. I remember how the family harvested breadfruit, plums, sugar apples, golden apples, pears (avocados), cherries, grapefruits, and limes. And they had the distinction of having the sole custard apple tree in the neighborhood. Additionally, Mr. Marshall had a much larger piece of land farther from the house that grew mainly sugar cane. So, the value he placed on hard work was never in doubt.

Nonetheless, Mr. Marshall was skillful in another area. He was a carpenter, who was under the watchful eye of many as he mastered his trade. He might have even vicariously passed on his love for what he did to his children. One of them told me the story about how she was working at putting a desk together, and his comment to her was that she looked like she knew what she was doing; obviously referring to the skills she had achieved from observing him at work.

In addition to being skillful at carpentry and building trades I have to credit him with the title of a trendsetter. He was the first in Roebuck to convert his house to the flat-top style. Because of his leadership, other residents did the same. Secondly, others followed his lead when he used a special color scheme to paint his house. Such was the character of the man. Who knows how many he has influenced for good without overtly trying, but by just being himself? I, along with all in Roebuck, was always grateful and happy to have had him as a mentor and an example.

My parents' value of respect for others was especially for the older people that lived in our Roebuck community. But that did not mean that we were free to disrespect others that lived beyond the boundaries in nearby Indian Ground, Four Hill, and any other place, for that matter. As long as they were living, breathing persons, it was our duty to show them respect and demonstrate good manners towards them. So, when I made my daily trek to Indian Ground to visit my maternal grandmother, I ensured that I was armed with my parents' respect protocol, ready to be deployed at a moment's notice.

In Indian Ground, there were specific individuals for whom I had an enormous amount of respect. I had no choice but to do so. Respect for them coursed through my veins. It was in my DNA. I am referring to my grandmother, Doris Worrell, her husband, Harold, and my Aunt Gloria, my maternal relatives. I could write pages about the love and respect that flowed between us. But all I will say here is that Harold was not my actual grandfather, and that anyone who did not know of our background would find it hard to believe that he wasn't, just by observing how he treated me. My grandmother was one of my favorite people, and Gloria is still the best aunt my siblings and I could ask for. I will probably write extensively about our relationship in a future project.

Eric Nicholls from Indian Ground, just over the hill from Roebuck, was another gentleman I respected and regarded highly, and he respected me in return. He was an influential lighthouse in every sense of the word. He lived well into his nineties, and even though he had been gone for a while, my memories of him are still fairly current and very much active. Everyone called him Brother Nick. So did I. I can't remember ever calling him Mr. Nicholls, even though the formality that my parents demanded was due him. And referring to him as Eric was out of the question. Brother Nick was a term of endearment and respect. He, too, was a churchman at the Indian Ground Christian Mission, and like my mother, it was evident that he, too, highly valued church attendance.

After my father migrated to the UK when I was around eleven years old, I could sense that Brother Nick was taking a keen interest in me and wanted to be sure that I had a male presence to replace the one that migrated with my father. Of course, he never communicated that in so many words, but his actions and comments spoke volumes to me as a kid. He always had an encouraging comment whenever we stopped to talk on the street. I always appreciated that he never appeared to be in a hurry and that the time he spent with me was well-spent.

When I started high school, I did not run into Brother Nick as often as before, but whenever he saw me, his questions and comments were directed at how I was doing in school. One of his regular questions was, "Are you doing your school lessons?" I appreciated that so much. The thought that he had taken an interest in how I was doing in school was a boost. And I made sure I had a good report to give him about my school marks whenever he asked.

Brother Nick would often take the time to ask about how my father was doing in England, and he appeared genuinely touched and concerned when my report was not all that good. It was usually difficult to talk about that, especially as I got older. And I could tell that he understood my discomfort. Above all, I always wanted to behave the right way when he saw me so as not to disappoint him. He was very observant concerning my adolescent growth spurt and would laughingly tell me, "Man, you're getting so tall. You will soon be as tall as me." I always appreciated that and felt a little grown up after that.

Soon after I started high school, I went to live with a school friend and his family in another parish, coming home only on weekends. I ran into him one such weekend, and he was so excited. "I heard your name on the radio. I was so happy," he told me. Of course, I knew exactly what he was talking about. I had recently done well in a cross-country race, and he congratulated me. It was impossible to put into words the impact Brother Nick's attention was having on me. It was the kind of impact that a son craves from his biological father. But Brother Nick stood in the gap and ensured I got the fatherly attention I needed.

As I write, I consider how fortunate I was, and still am, to have had the fortune of men like Brother Nick to step up and provide for the need I had, and that so many like me had, and still have. I mentioned the part played by my 'grandfather' and my uncles Wilfred, Percival (Brown Boy), and James (Son) also did their part. They were family and behaved like a family where I was concerned. And I am eternally grateful for the guidance, the presence, and the attention when I needed them most. But Brother Nick was not family. He simply saw a need and filled a need. How could I not be respectful?

Brother Nick was happy for me when I started teaching right out of high school. I remember him putting his hand on my shoulder and telling me that he was proud of me and that he knew my mother was as well. He continued to ask about my father, but by this time, the news about him and our relationship was still not good. He would listen and understand. In one of our chats, I announced that I would be going to teachers' college. He was so excited, so much so that a casual passerby who was unaware of our relationship probably would have thought that I was his son. He was so happy for me.

I went to see him before I left for college in Jamaica. "More school again?" he beamed. I was back in Barbados only briefly after spending three years in Jamaica and did not get to see him before going off to The Virgin Islands to teach. I had been gone from Barbados for over forty years, but I always made it my duty to visit him whenever I was back.

The last time I saw him, it was clear that the years had taken a toll, and that he was not as alert as he used to be. Initially, he did not remember me, but we had a lively discussion after his wife, Viterose, reminded him, "It is Sylester, Iola's son." He wanted to know how I was doing and if I still lived in America. I managed to squeeze out a few words of thanks before I left. I truly respected Brother Nick for filling a void at the right time. He has since passed on, but the memories are fresh, even to this day.

You may have already realized that I have had, and still have, a lot of respect for several people, especially males, that have made an impression and a positive impact on my life. I firmly believe that I accepted their influence because I was missing that male presence in my home after my father migrated and my mother was raising us independently. But it has to be stated that at no time did any of the men mentioned so far ever told me that they were doing what they were doing because they wanted to fill in for my absent father.

Furthermore, I believe that they were not even conscious of the influence they were shedding, and that their work on my behalf was unplanned and natural. As a matter of fact, I had already earned their respect, and they mine, before my father's departure. And secondly, it is fair to theorize that they might have similarly influenced other youngsters in our neighborhood in one way or another.

I do not mean to send the message that I did not respect the women of Roebuck when I was growing up. Far from it. Or those from Indian Ground, Four Hill, or any nearby villages. Or that they did not respect me. My respect was evenly distributed across gender, age, and other demographic classifications. But it would be remiss of me and utterly disrespectful if I fail to at least mention those women who poured everything they had into me. I have already mentioned those that were closest to me. My mother is single-handedly responsible for who I am, who we (my siblings and I) are today, and for the achievements and success, we have been able to reap.

Ultimately, she was the one that enforced the values that are the focus of this work, and for both mothering and fathering the five of us. My grandmother, my mother's mother, Mama, as she was affectionately named, got all the respect she deserved and more. Not only because she made sure that I ate at her house every evening but because she was also faithful at enforcing and modeling the values that were important. And, of course, my aunt, Gloria, who still deserves the respect she receives from all of us. She has always been a staple in our lives and is highly appreciated for what she has done and continues to do with us and for us. And I dare not forget my four sisters, Elaine, Yvonne, Cheryl, and Heather, who I am sure were the first to provide the hands-on training I needed regarding respecting women.

But it takes a village. That's the maxim my mother probably had in mind when deciding that the value of respect for others was a priority for her. And for us. And the Roebuck village was populated by watchful, protective, and even corrective females. I might forget some names, but my memory lapse is not an indication of a lack of respect toward anyone. Still, the following list readily comes to mind: Ms. Morris (Halls), who is still alive at 102, Ms. Watson, Aunt Rita, Ms. Marshall, Ms. Scantlebury, Sister Sobers, Rita, Joycelyn, Ms. Blackman, Ms. Straker, Ms. Gilkes, Ms. Headley, Ms. Nurse, Ms. Cox, Ms. Griffith, and Ms. Rhoda. Ms. Halls and Rita are the only ones in this celebrated group who are still alive, and who I continue to respect, even from such a long distance. I make it a point of duty to visit them whenever I am back in Roebuck.

But after paying limited but respectful tribute to the women mentioned above, I am returning to identify another gentleman that meant so much to me and to whom I was grateful, thankful, and respectful. Mr. Vaughn was not from Roebuck, and I have to thank my friend, Lelia, for planting the idea in my consciousness to look outside Roebuck for someone I respected. Her very words were, "Look outside. Make it wider than just Roebuck." As a matter of fact, her father, Brother Nick, that I profiled above, was also not from Roebuck but from Indian Ground, a neighboring district.

I briefly and casually mentioned Mr. Vaughn in a previous chapter, deciding to wait for a more appropriate time to expand on my professional respect for him. I started teaching right out of high school, just after a month or so, at the local psychiatric hospital, where I was in the nurses' trainee program. I quickly realized that this was not the direction I wanted to pursue. I submitted my application to teach and was more than delighted when I landed a position at All Saints Boys School because the school had a reputation for having very good teachers and was well known for its success in turning out students that were successful in the eleven-plus exam that I mentioned earlier.

But All Saints had much more than good teaching experts in Mr. Hinkson, Mr. Benn, Mr. Griffith, Mr. Hal Edwards, Mr. Springer, Martin Ramsay, Vasco Toppin, Francilla Haynes, and of course, my good friend, Tony Jordan. It had a superbly phenomenal principal and leader, Mr. Charles Vaughn. When I started teaching, I was a nervous and insecure wreck. And Mr. Vaughn recognized that. My class was right under his nose, just a few steps down from the platform where he worked from his desk, and obviously observing my insecurity at the same time. I could hear Vasco Toppin and Rudolph Odwin, both young teachers like myself, sounding so confident and in control across the large one-room space. But I was the opposite, so much so that I could feel the sweat running down my body.

One day, I was teaching multiplication to my Class Three students when Mr. Vaughn stepped down from his position on the platform, rested his hand on my shoulder, and uttered the most comforting sentiment I have ever heard in my teaching career that has spanned some forty-seven years. "It is going to be alright," he encouraged. I remember him taking the chalk and teaching the class, walking me through the steps of teaching the concept. He did it so politely and professionally that even the students thought nothing of it. He advised me to be confident and strong and how to engage the students by asking them questions and giving them the opportunity to solve some problems on their own instead of me lecturing all the time. He returned to his desk and observed me teach, giving me the occasional nod of approval. My confidence grew rapidly as Mr. Vaughn continued to give me tips on how to teach.

Two things come to mind as I write this account. First, Mr. Vaughn was way ahead of his time. Currently, the practice is for lead teachers to go into classrooms and demonstrate teaching methods to teachers. Mr. Vaughn was practicing this kind of intervention way back in the sixties.

Secondly, I had read an article a while back that referenced research that concluded that many teachers leave the profession within three years for reasons that may be surprising; the major one being the lack of administrative support. I could have been one of those teachers, especially considering my insecurity and timidity. But because of Mr. Vaughn's intervention on my behalf, I did not become a statistic, but went on to experience a lengthy career in education as a teacher and principal, and university professor. It goes without saying that his influence was powerful in helping me decide to be a principal and put in place similar interventions for young teachers.

But Mr. Vaughn was not through with me just yet. He saw that I, and other young and inexperienced teachers needed more work and polishing if we were to flourish and be the best we could be. Just like the ones I mentioned earlier. And his next professional and training intervention encouraged me to respect him even more.

My friend, Tony Jordan, will appreciate this because we have talked and laughed about some of the occurrences during this very helpful professional development activity. But on the serious side, Mr. Vaughn, from time to time, would arrange demonstration lessons in which young teachers like me would teach a class with the entire staff observing, to provide feedback, commendations, and recommendations. I wouldn't say I liked this initially, but it was one of the most helpful professional development experiences I could ask for. He purposely transformed the school into a laboratory and training institute to grow young teachers, so much so that when I finally went to teachers' college, I was a much stronger teacher, with a comfort level and security that I did not have before. I was ready for teaching practice (student teaching), approaching it with confidence and self-assurance.

And as if he had not done enough to earn my respect, Mr. Vaughn had one more respect-earning shot to unleash: one that I referred to earlier. And one for which I was totally unprepared. One day out of the blue, he asked, "So, when are you going to Erdiston (College}?" I must have mumbled a response of some sort, but was more surprised and humbled that he had seen potential and promise in me, when I had not given that much thought to my future at the time.

At the time, I knew that I wanted to continue teaching but had not yet thought about college. I am not absolutely clear, but if memory serves me correctly, he was very involved in my college application process, including securing the necessary application forms. He was probably saying to himself that he was responsible for my growth to this point, so why not see me through to the end? Now fifty or so years later, I am a retired teacher after an amazing and satisfying career. I could not find the words to thank him then, and even now, my respect for him for his contribution to my professional achievements is unsurpassed. He was truly a professional lighthouse that guided me and many others on our professional journey.

<u>Extended Value-added Thinking and Action:</u>

1. Make a list of all the people you respected as a youth and write a brief summary of how each one impacted you and why you respect them so much. Share your writing with each person.

2. Make a list of those people you think have a level of respect for you. Why do you think they respect you?

3. Make a list of persons that did not, or do not, earn your respect. Explain why the persons listed have not earned your respect.

4. Make another list of persons you think have not or do not respect you? Think about reasons why they do not respect you. What can you do to correct the situation and earn their respect?

5. Have you ever lost respect for anyone? Explain why. What has been done to restore the relationship?

6. Make a list of your personal qualities, skills, and expertise that endear you to others. How do you use them to influence others and earn their respect?

7. Make a list of those people you think have a level of respect for you. Why do you think they respect you?

8. Make a list of persons that did not, or do not, earn your respect. Explain why the persons listed have not earned your respect.

Chapter 6
A Piece of the Rock

A house is made of bricks and beams. A home is made of hopes and dreams

– Author Unknown

In the previous chapters, I discussed in great detail four values that my parents, and other Roebuck parents, held close and how they worked hard to make sure that those values became our values and be of benefit to us. Those were the significant values. The major values, so to speak. This suggests that there are, or were, other values as well. Not that those mentioned in this chapter are of less importance or minor significance. The reality is that the four previous ones were fundamental, with a major purpose to shape us into successful, respectful, independent, and productive citizens. However, these other values are just as meaningful and just as significant, even though they were not discussed as much as they were demonstrated and practiced.

My parents, especially my mother, placed a tremendous value on homeownership. As mentioned above, she did not talk about it much, or not at all. But it was evident that owning a piece of the rock, so to speak, was vitally important to her and the other homeowners in the Roebuck community where we lived.

I am sure that my mention of homeownership conjures up certain images in your mind regarding the kind of homes I am referencing. I have mentioned that ours was a small agricultural community, so you must have already concluded that our homes were not palatial or sprawling. And they were not. But the effort made by these proud residents to secure a home and maintain it on a meager income was a lesson of value.

Like the other houses in the neighborhood, ours was a small wooden structure with a front house (living room), a back house (family room/den), and two small bedrooms. As time went on, additions were made as finances became available, and as my mother's quest for something better grew larger and larger. It is apparent that her unspoken mantra was 'something better.' Just as it had always been as far as her other values were concerned.

It was not a matter of her being dissatisfied or discontented with her current housing situation. Far from it. Contentment was one of her most admired traits of character. Her attitude towards all of this appeared to have emerged from a covert belief and personal philosophy that if better is achievable, then better is worth pursuing. She was not a competitive person by nature, and I admired her carefulness not to yield to the temptation to live beyond her means or to keep up with the proverbial Joneses. Still, she would never sit idly by and watch her value, investment, and property deteriorate to a standard or a condition that was substandard by Roebuck standards or to one that was inferior when compared to the others that were neighbors.

Astounding is the apt way to describe her dogged approach to owning a space to call her own. And what is even more astonishing is the fact that the house spot (lot) on which the house was built was not even hers. Like my mom, the other owners that worked on the plantation did not own the land. It wasn't theirs. Still, they built on it. It belonged to the plantation, and they paid a nominal fee to rent it. The cost to own it probably would have been prohibitive, but I am positive that they would have moved heaven and earth to secure the plot if the option had been presented to them. They would have approached the matter with just as much focus and with the same level of seriousness that they did for the other values they embraced.

As was the case with the other values my mother held dear, she was not satisfied with the bare minimum. By this time, she was in charge of maintaining the house since my father had already migrated to the UK. She was now the leader in every facet of parenting, home building, family building, and last but by no means least, house improvement. And she didn't take the responsibility lightly. She was in charge of a growing family, and as far as she was concerned, the present space was inadequate. Something better was her silent mantra. Owning a house was not enough. Owning a house with adequate space was the ideal.

Even though homeownership was the primary value, the spin-off value and the one that was most appreciated and respected was the one that my mother and the other homeowners in Roebuck prized the most: that the house was much more than a building; that it was meant to be a place of refuge, security, and protection for those she valued beyond any other thing – her children.

Having a space that was dedicated as a place of retreat and a haven for us was a priceless value. So, the pride and the care that my mother poured into the house were huge and understandable; just as huge as if it were an expansive and rambling mansion on a high hill. She employed every resource to maintain it in a condition that was homely. There was no lack of human resources to accomplish the heavy lifting. My siblings and I were the hired hands to do the heavy lifting to make it shine, especially the front house – an appropriate reference to the value she placed on work that was mentioned previously. It was always painted inside and out and refreshed at Christmastime.

Overtly, it was as if owning a house was a project that brought her satisfaction and a sense of accomplishment and ownership. She and the other owners kept their homestead in a state of repair and worked purposefully and proudly to fix a leaky roof and replace a rotting board, with their pride keeping them from allowing their investment to diminish into a state of shabbiness and disorder.

I have previously mentioned that the word mortgage was never mentioned in casual conversation, or in any conversation, for that matter. It was not needed. It was not listed among the spelling words that schoolchildren were assigned. It was not even a word they could employ their phonetic skills to decipher, spell, or write correctly. One hundred percent homeownership took care of that.

Homeownership was recognized as such a huge value among the residents that it made specific terms that are associated with today's bustling housing market and thriving building industry null and void. Industry terms like rent, down payment, and apartment, were never a part of the local language simply because there was no use for them. Even for sale or for rent signs were never a part of the local landscape. The locals held on to their houses. They valued their houses, and they were determined to permanently enjoy them to the end.

As such, there were never church prayers going up in the Pentecost Church down the road for Sister This or Brother That, who could not keep up with their mortgage payments and were in danger of losing their home to a big commercial bank in the city.

The value of homeownership and building them from the ground up, and even moving them from one spot to the next with the aid of local craftsmen, was the order of the day.

As mentioned above, some homeowners in Roebuck moved their houses from one place to the next. Plainly put, they moved their value with them. This does not mean to convey the message that this was a regular practice or that they were nomadic or transitory in any way. For the most part, almost one hundred percent of the structures remained in their original location for a lifetime. But what this moving situation does support is the fact that conditions arose from time to time that necessitated such a move. And one has to understand that the only reason such a move was made was to cement the value of homeownership and to improve the standard of living of those occupying the residence.

People didn't simply wake up and decide to move their house to another location. To this day, the vast majority of the houses remain in the exact location as they were when I was a boy growing up there and are still occupied by those that inherited the value of homeownership that was passed on to them by the original value originators. It was not like them to move from house to house, or to buy and sell, as is the case in some markets today. Stability, contentment, and satisfaction were the components of the value they built from the ground up.

Still, it was an amazing event to watch as workmen quickly and easily disassembled a dwelling, loaded it onto a lorry, transported it to its new location, and with the same degree of expertise, put it together again, just as quickly as they had taken it apart. I watched this happen more than once but was never invited to participate or felt obliged to volunteer, as was the case with other forms of work that were discussed in a previous chapter. This was probably because I, and others like me, were too young at the time and did not possess the technical capability needed to do the job efficiently.

Obviously, the houses that were the object and subject of the value of homeownership that our parents held, were simply built and constructed of building materials that were not the sturdiest available. Our mother's house was a board (wood) house, as were all the others in Roebuck. Still, it was her castle. Her value. Wall houses, built from bricks or concrete, or stone, had not yet made their way to our community. But now they have. The opposite is now the norm. The standard and the value have been upgraded. I was pleased to discover that existing houses that were around when I was a youngster have been upgraded and retrofitted with the more sturdy and affluent building materials like concrete, cinder blocks, and stone, to reflect a more modern and diversity of styles that were not common when I was a lad.

To be exact, there was one structure at the top of my gap that was constructed from a blackish-colored stone. It was there before anybody in Roebuck was born. It was the only house in the neighborhood not made of wood. Orrie and her large family lived in the cramped space. I am unsure if she owned it or how she came by it, but on one of my visits to Roebuck, after I had been living in the US for some time, I discovered that the house was no longer there. I didn't inquire about the method of demolition used to destroy the queer-looking house or why it was removed, but I later learned that it was used to house slaves back in the day.

So, it didn't matter the nature of the building materials that were used to construct those places of abode. The value my mother and the other residents of Roebuck placed in homeownership had nothing to do with wood, or concrete, or stone but everything to do with owning a space to call their own; a space they could look at with pride and satisfaction, a space that was theirs to provide for the safety of themselves and their children. Securing a piece of the rock and living the Barbados dream was the driving force that energized their value of homeownership. They ably demonstrated that owning a home and the security and prestige it brought were not reserved for those of a certain class, education level, or one's station in life. It was an absolutely first-class lesson in how they prioritized homeownership over other collectibles that they could have mustered.

It appears they made a conscious and collective decision early on to invest in a home instead of expensive clothing, designer jewelry, and classic automobiles. In fact, there were only one or two cars in the whole neighborhood. Mr. Scantlebury, the shopkeeper, owned one, and I think Pastor Sobers had one later. They appeared to have learned the important lessons in appreciation and depreciation from the outset. Apparently, owning a home was a fair substitute for some of the finer material and immaterial belongings they did not possess.

But even though my mother valued homeownership as much as she did, she looked at this value in a one-dimensional way. Though she appeared to have been self-educated concerning the concepts of appreciation and depreciation, she did not conceive of value in terms of resale value. She did not repair her house and maintain it in an attractive appearance solely because the resale value would be elevated or tripled after many years. Her sole purpose and dream was to remain in her home permanently.

Consequently, I never heard her speak of resale value, or of keeping the house as a return on her investment to provide for her in her golden years, or to build wealth over time, to amass equity, or as a tax write-off when she filed their taxes, even though I never heard her talk about filing taxes or anything of the sort. Her value of homeownership went deeper than that. Much deeper. It had nothing to do with future money or financial security. It had everything to do with her satisfaction of owning something that was useful, secure, and lasting for her and her family. That was her equity and her value. Home was where her heart was, so to speak. It was the dignity and pride that went along with homeownership.

As I write this, I can't help but reflect on one or more factors that figured largely in the grand scheme of things, as to why my mother and the others in Roebuck valued owning their own homes. Primarily, the houses they owned were built for security, shelter, and sanctuary for their families. But from everything I observed, and from the details I can recall, there appeared to be an added function and value. This added value was never voiced or discussed, but it was evident that the houses in my neighborhood also functioned as centers of entertainment and visitation. And what is my proof? I have hard data. Though not statistical, it is factual data that is personal to me as well.

It was not uncommon for neighbors to show up uninvited and without prior warning just to casually visit, to just talk and spend time in each other's homes. Entertainment may be a strong term that I am using to describe these loosely social events. There was no drinking or music or dancing or the other social goings-on that are usually associated with entertainment, but it was entertainment, nonetheless.

And they didn't gather to watch their favorite television show because the technology had not yet come to those parts, and electricity had not yet made its way to the neighborhood. But there was talk and laughter in abundance, not of a mischievous or gossipy type, but lighthearted chatter that cemented friendships and strengthened bonds of camaraderie that held the safety and strength of the neighborhood together.

And there was usually food. Those women shared what they had without question, and it was the neighborhood practice to serve a bowl of chicken soup, or a plate of rice and peas with saltfish or flying fish gravy, or stew food served with red herring sauce to those that showed up when food was being dished out from the pot. Ms. Watson would drop by to talk on occasion. Ms. Morris would do the same. And Cadogan would come by. And my mother would return the unannounced visits when it was her turn. It was a kind of open-door policy, with the understanding that mi casa es su casa. I have to tell you that these unannounced visits were not reserved for the women of the neighborhood. Kids got in on the action as well. I know I did. But for a completely different purpose.

I was on a zoom chat with my cousins, Henson and Keith, in the UK. Lyndell, Don, and Michael, who also reside in the UK, were on the call as well. We had a good laugh recalling the habit and expertise we had as boys, knowing precisely when food was being served at the neighbor's house and how we would make a timely visit just to get a share of food. We were good 'pot timers,' a title we appropriately conferred on ourselves. The most important detail concerning this community practice was the understanding that it was okay and accepted. Ms. Morris didn't mind me showing up at dinner time. It was her pleasure to give me something to eat. And my mother didn't mind Henson suddenly appearing when it was time to eat. To them, it had nothing to do with the food but with the fact that they, as homeowners, had a space that was available to provide welcome and service to others.

Like the other values detailed earlier, my mother's value of homeownership had its incidental teaching lessons; lessons that I later believed were instilled in us without direct instruction or teachings. She never sat us down and instructed us on how to own our own house once we were grown, or provided lessons on the value and importance of owning one. But observing the effort and care she and the others in

Roebuck invested in the upkeep of their homes was enough to plant the seed of the value of homeownership as a goal for the future. Neither my siblings nor I owned a house before we left Roebuck, but once we arrived in the US, and were sufficiently financially stable, the desire to purchase a house was automatic. Making a long story short and skipping the details on our personal homeownership experiences, the conclusion is that each of us had decided to make owning our own homes a priority, a value which my mother so ably demonstrated.

Continuing with the theme mentioned above, I think I am correct in concluding that my mother's value of homeownership has impacted us more than we would care to believe. And I can't even recall not wanting to purchase a home once I was settled on where I wanted to live in the US, and was financially able. The fact is that, along with my wife, we made it a joint purpose to be financially able. It became a priority above every other family plan. It was the natural and normal way to think; a value that was probably motivated by the experience to which we had become accustomed back home.

As mentioned before, my mother and the other residents in Roebuck were homeowners outright. They did not pay rent to a landlord. Neither were they migratory in the sense that they packed up and moved ever so often because they could not financially afford to remain in a dwelling that was not theirs. Obviously, we noticed this and came away with the idea that homeownership was a right, a dignity, and an enormous value.

So, it should not be a huge surprise that the drive to own a house once we were in the US was so ingrained in our psyche, and that it was pursued with such a quiet intensity, that it caught the attention of others. Some even took the time to remark on the quickness and the drive that propelled immigrants like me, to have realized one aspect of the American dream with such alarming speed, zeal, and determination;

so much so that they were moved to voice their bewilderment in words of surprise, or disbelief. My reaction to their concern was that they were grossly unaware that it was my mother's value of homeownership actively at work behind the scenes.

It was not as if my US colleagues, associates, and friends did not own their own homes. Most of them did. But they were caught off guard at the spectacle of immigrants from another culture that is usually described as third world or developing, or even monikered later as 'shit hole countries,' making such focused and rapid strides towards the value of homeownership in a foreign and adopted home. And so, the questions so often verbalized were of this nature: Already? How did he do that so quickly? That big house is yours? These are the same questions that usually follow when people like me achieve high levels of advanced education, climb to the top rounds of the corporate ladder, or achieve envious professional recognition in science, medicine, research, influence, and leadership.

Coincidentally, the state of affairs mentioned in the scenario just described, is a perfect illustration of the values of education, making use of opportunities, hard work, church attendance, respect, and homeownership, coalescing into a broad and value system.

My response to such statements and queries, whether or not they are voiced as positive and congratulatory sentiments or otherwise, has always been rooted in the discussion and beliefs that I have attempted to explore in the previous pages of this chapter – that the value of homeownership was treasured by my mother; that it was not only cultural but necessary; and that she and her associates, poor and uneducated plantation workers, carpenters, and general laborers, were sophisticated enough to even think of owning a home outright. And that wrapped up in the value of homeownership were the qualities of pride, dignity, and the originator of a space to house the security, safety, and comfort for family and others.

In concluding this expose on my mother's value of homeownership, and how it impacted my siblings and me, quietly driving us to adopt her value, I have to mention that in her quest to achieve and personalize her value, that competition of any measure ever entered the equation. She was not driven by personal victories and selfish priorities that turned her into a fierce competitor, vying for the first prize or a gold medal for having been the first to own a house or to be recognized for having the biggest or best one in the neighborhood. I can't bring myself to imagine her engaging in such a duel. That basal thinking and outrageous behavior was not integral to her value of homeownership. It was foreign to who she was as a person, and value-keeper.

The undeniable fact is that she appeared to support and encourage others in a common endeavor, helping as best she could at lending a hand to set up or even move a house to another location in the small neighborhood, as was mentioned before. Just like they came together in a united force to harvest each other's sugar cane when the occasion rolled around on an annual basis.

But it goes without saying that the homeownership value had an even more valuable outcome. It created a bond that created a strong sense of neighborhood security, protection, and friendship. The unwritten agreement that was honored and appreciated by all, was enshrined in the belief that homeownership was the correct value on which to build a safe and protected neighborhood.

<u>Extended Value-added Thinking and Action:</u>

1. Did your parents own their own home when you were growing up? What conversations did you hear between them regarding owning their own home?

2. Make a list of the people in the neighborhood where you grew up that owned the house in which they lived. Was this a minority or majority number?

3. Do you own your own home? When did you decide that owning your own home was important? What did your parents consciously or unconsciously teach you about homeownership?

4. Apart from the financial investment, what are some of the other long-term benefits that you have personally experienced as a result of owning your home?

5. List some of the challenges you and others experienced or are experiencing in pursuing homeownership? What steps did you take to deal with those challenges?

6. Complete one of the following statements:

I own a home because…

I would like to own my own home because….

Epilogue

It took me a long time to complete this project after I began working on it soon after I returned from Barbados in 2016. The fact is that I shelved it after the initial attempt, picking it up only intermittently. The urge to finish it recently returned with a vengeance, along with the energy, will, and determination lacking from the outset. I often say to friends and acquaintances that I would starve if I were an author that wrote for a living, meaning that even though I have authored two previous books, the dedication and the motivation to write regularly showed up only every now and then.

Fortunately, this writing experience has been personally rewarding on several fronts. For a long time, I have often wondered if some or all of the values that shaped my youth, those expectations that my mother and the others put in place and set up as standards, are still respected and held in high regard among the current youth in my former district. It is rather difficult to satisfy my curiosity simply because I have not been back for a considerable time to observe and gather anecdotal data. Neither have I nor anyone else conducted scientific research to answer the basic question.

However, during my most recent visit, I observed enough to conclude that at least some of the values discussed were still alive, if only partially. It was evident that the place had changed drastically, particularly regarding the number of youth and teenagers, compared to when I was growing up in that setting and in the atmosphere discussed in the discourse. The narrow street that was once crowded with flocks and herds of sheep and cows, shepherded by half-awake, half-asleep early-teen boys, was now uncluttered and uncrowded. And the familiar culture of grown men and women hurrying in the early morning air to their jobs in the fields of the plantation was long gone.

Most disturbing of all was that the music created by the enjoyment of children playing cricket in the street during the day and hide and seek when the sun was about to set, particularly in the summertime when they were on holiday, was now silent. Equally disappointing was the noticeable absence of children, period. The one-time practice of the young ones going to shop at Ms. Watson's to trust lard oil, salt bread, red herring, and kerosene was outdated and dead, partly due to the fact that the shop was closed for business and had been closed for a long time. It has to be mentioned that there were other mitigating circumstances that were responsible, including a noticeably higher standard of living.

Still, the strong impression was that the flat screen, the X-box, cable television, and Netflix were now relatively readily available and preferred. I was so devastated by the absence of children that in a conversation with my sister, Elaine, I made the statement that the community was dying, a prediction based on the observation that many of the seniors that were the dispensers of values and culture had passed on, and the few that were still alive were not in a position to teach, and model as was their role when I was a youngster. Additionally, another observation is worth mentioning. Females of childbearing age were few, some already having given birth years before, while others might have decided against motherhood. I raised the above assertions to support my position that the indigenous culture and the values that were the order of the day a few generations previous were now on life support simply because of the unfortunate state of affairs mentioned above: the dwindling numbers of young people, and a similar situation where older residents are concerned. One example will suffice. One which is the most glaring, simply because it was a setting that was so simple, yet an absolutely perfect classroom to teach and learn some of the basic values discussed in this project.

Before the availability of running water in the homes in Roebuck, young and old alike gathered at a central spot in the neighborhood to collect water from a public standpipe under The Marshalls spreading breadfruit tree. It was the perfect setting for the youth to practice their respect value by greeting the seniors with a good morning or evening, as the case might have been. Or even with a hearty thank you for receiving help hoisting a heavy bucket of water to the head. Or a smile of gratitude to a youth for picking a ripened breadfruit for an older resident that was too old to climb the tree. It was a simple but appropriate outdoor classroom for reinforcing the value of respect. But the classroom is no longer, for obvious reasons discussed above. Recently, I received some sad news from my cousin, Dorcas. The breadfruit tree had suddenly fallen. No rain, storm, or hurricane winds. It perpetuated the place's culture and established a setting for reinforcing some of the important and vital values. I was more than a little touched by the number of people that commented on the news and shared pictures of the fallen food supply with me. It was as if a member of the neighborhood had passed away.

While there were little or no sightings of youth attending church in the numbers that I was used to, it was evident that some had taken the value of homeownership seriously. And there was also evidence that one or more had decided to put the value of making use of opportunities to the test by setting up a small business and taking the step into the world of entrepreneurship. Additionally, others had decided to take the deep dive by valuing education. A number had completed high school and were employed as civil servants, while others had gone to university and graduated as teachers, doctors, and lawyers.

The conclusion is that my mother and her cohorts consciously decided on a set of values geared to secure their children's future. They should be recognized, remembered, and honored for their unselfish gift to their community.

Readers' Comments and Insights

"An excellent discourse on how values taught and caught in the home and supported and complemented by the 'village' have impact for a lifetime."

Randall Phillips, MBA, Federal Auditor (retired)

"It is intensely fascinating to consider the significant role that values play in our lives, from appreciating hard (real) work to undertaking the risk of the unknown, mixed with education (learning) and respect for our elders. This treatise explores the roles of values on every level in the life of its author; quite a sharp distinction from the safety and protective privilege that today's younger generation enjoys in its reluctance to engage in "adulting" (assuming responsibility)."

Lionel Lynch, MBA, Strategic Source Manager

"This book transported me to a place of reflection on my own life and the values that are important to me. I was intrigued by the clear insights Dr. Carrington extracted from each value, and was grateful for the tasks he proposed at the end of each chapter. It is absolutely inspiring."

Ingrid Jones, Ph.D., Professional Learning Coordinator, Catoosa

County Public Schools.

"Dr. Carrington has captured and woven together the stories of his early childhood to draw a beautiful portrait of the character of the people who helped shape his life. The strong values instilled, ultimately pushed him to positively impact others."

Leila Nicholls-Springer, Founder and president of The Olive Branch of Hope

"This book on values provides an eloquent and captivating journey through the eyes of Dr. Carrington. Each chapter captures his mother's brilliant illustrations and life lessons, equipping the reader with essential success factors. What a remarkable way to document her exceptional legacy via these life-changing nuggets. Dr. Carrington has managed to elevate these values into his personal and professional experiences. Be inspired!"

Kathy Purnell, Ph.D., Senior Advisor to the president, Southern Adventist University

"The maternal effect insightfully and eloquently captures the values instilled in Dr. Carrington by his mother and her contemporaries. A beautiful picture is painted in this work of childhood growth and development into adulthood that was buttressed by impermeable and priceless values. You see and smell the plants of his mother's garden planted in the east of their home to capture the best sunlight. You experience with chills the rhythm and excitement of those early church services…. As an educator, he instructs in this work in a manner that places readers squarely in the place of his upbringing and transports them to where those values have taken him today. This work will be beneficial to a wide cross-section of multiple generations. Its principles are timeless. Its values are transformational and practical.

John Mills, D. Min, Pastor

About the Author

D r. Sylvester Carrington was born in Barbados, where he completed his education through high school and teacher's college. He is a retired educator with extensive teaching and administrative experience at all levels of private, public, and college education. He is also the author of *A Principal's Personal Journey and It's Your Word Against Mine.* He and his wife, Hortense, are the parents of three adult sons and two grandchildren. Dr. Carrington can be reached at lionel49.c@gmail.com.